THE SHOOTING SCRIPT®

TAKING WOODSTOCK

THE SHOOTING SCRIPT®

TAKING WOODSTOCK

SCREENPLAY AND INTRODUCTION BY
JAMES SCHAMUS

FOREWORD BY
ANG LEE

A Newmarket Shooting Script® Series Book
NEWMARKET PRESS • NEW YORK

FIRST EDITION

10   9   8   7   6   5   4   3   2   1

ISBN: 978-1-55704-847-9

Library of Congress Catalog-in-Publication Data available upon request.

QUANTITY PURCHASES

Companies, professional groups, clubs, and other organizations may qualify for special terms when ordering quantities of this title. For information e-mail sales@newmarketpress.com or write to Special Sales, Newmarket Press, 18 East 48th Street, New York, NY 10017; call (212) 832-3575 ext. 19 or 1-800-669-3903; FAX (212) 832-3629.

Website: www.newmarketpress.com

Manufactured in the United States of America.

OTHER BOOKS IN THE NEWMARKET SHOOTING SCRIPT® SERIES INCLUDE:

OTHER NEWMARKET PICTORIAL MOVIEBOOKS AND NEWMARKET INSIDER FILM BOOKS INCLUDE:

CONTENTS

FOREWORD

BY ANG LEE

Late in his life, Buddha gathered his disciples around him. They wanted to hear his final words of wisdom, but he wouldn't say anything. Then he picked up a flower and showed it to them. They didn't understand. But one of his disciples, Mahakashyapa, broke into a smile when he saw the flower. Buddha told him he was the one who understood the meaning of this "Flower Sermon," a meaning that couldn't be put in words, and told him he would be the first master to carry on the teachings of Buddhism.

Maybe the Buddha was among us while we were making *Taking Woodstock*, but we were too happy to notice. Unlike all my other movies, I myself didn't suffer during the making of it, so I really have nothing of interest or meaning to say about it. Like most people, when I'm happy I'm not so interesting. I think, however, the film might be somewhat interesting, even though there's nothing meaningful to be found in it. Now that the film is done, I am happy to say the screenplay already means nothing to me. The film, too, will blow in the wind for a while, and then it will be nothing, if it isn't already. But maybe all this nothing will make you smile.

—May 2009

INTRODUCTION

BY JAMES SCHAMUS

*B*eing here, at Woodstock, now.

Woodstock, of course, didn't happen at Woodstock; it happened at Bethel, New York, apparently in August 1969. To *be* at Woodstock was thus to be in the *idea* of Woodstock, but somewhere else than Woodstock. If you were in Woodstock in mid-August 1969, you weren't *there*.

Woodstock was an *event*, that is to say, something that didn't just actually happen, but an *actuality* that came into being, when something—when many things—happened. A human actuality is a possibility that is immanent in us as a kind of freedom—and the event that represents that actuality to us is never simply identical to the specific temporal-spatial confluence with which history tries to pin it down. That's why events like Woodstock are meaningful—the *happening* of them is not just the same thing as what happened at a specific place and time; nor are such events merely "symbolic" representations of abstract ideas, for they have a reality that, in important ways, exceeds mere fact or image.

Hence the hidden truth in the adage "If you can remember Woodstock, you weren't there." Because, no matter how drug-soaked your memories, even if you were there, there and then, the act of remembering—that is, the affixing of the experience to a specific temporal-spatial locus—circumscribes the event, makes of it a fact, more than an actuality. But for us to realize that actuality, we must somehow *return* there.

Thus the paradox: to let Woodstock continue to be an actuality, so that we can be here with it, now, we must remember enough to want to go back there, then. What is *possible* is, of necessity, *past*.

This paradox was very present to the Woodstock generation itself, inextricably tied to the "innocence" we associate with the event. It was and still is often expressed in "Eastern," Zen-style language, but the conception of time Woodstock invokes is also very Judeo-Christian: to take the journey to Max Yasgur's farm was, as Joni Mitchell put it, to "get back to the garden," that is, to the Eden before the creation of human history and time whose origins are, in Milton's words, our "first disobedience." Human freedom—which Richie Havens so memorably and spontaneously praised in song at Woodstock—exists only in human time, a kind of temporality that owes its existence to original sin.

To tell the story of the event that is Woodstock is, necessarily, to follow narrative modes and conventions that treat the happenings of human history as unfolding in some kind of causal order. We assume that when we choose to narrate that one thing happened after another thing, we mean to understand that the earlier thing participated in the causes of the later thing. A "good" story often foregrounds the seemingly trivial details that later, surprisingly, turn out to have been "causes" for the story's denouement.

In narrating *Taking Woodstock*, though, we embraced a chain of events that were as accidental as they were causal; indeed, it is precisely the openness to and acceptance of accident that so inspires us about the Woodstock generation; and any proper narrative of that event should try as best it can to embody that openness. The scholar Gary

Saul Morson, in his *Narrative and Freedom*, has written beautifully about how narratives need not "destroy the openness of time," but can embrace contingency—and thus freedom—by creating what he calls a "plurality of temporalities."

If our modest approach to storytelling in *Taking Woodstock* is not quite ambitious enough to live up to Morson's main examples (Tolstoy and Dostoevsky are his literary heroes), in a small way we still want to contribute to the unfolding story of freedom that is the Woodstock story. To do so, we kept to the margins, to "a" story about Woodstock rather than "the" story, to a peripheral sphere where the center of the meaning of Woodstock could be found, in a sense, outside the defining circle.

And so happenstance brings us the story of Elliot Tiber, the son of the owners of the El Monaco Motel, who happened to be there then, and who made a phone call to Woodstock producer Mike Lang, inviting him to come to his family's motel in White Lake, New York, after hearing that the neighboring town of Wallkill had pulled the permit on the festival. Did that phone call lead *directly* to Max Yasgur's farm, three miles down the road from the El Monaco? Every participant involved remembers the chain of events differently, but no matter. It was a call that, in Elliot's wonderful telling, served as a tiny crack in an edifice that, a month later, would spectacularly tumble, revealing to him a new, alternative reality that catalyzed his own—and millions of people's—search for freedom.

Part of that alternative reality is the story of the pioneering lesbian, gay, bi, and (as we now name it) transgender communities that formed an integral part of the Woodstock Nation, but whose roles have been effaced under the weight of a dominant, primarily straight image of sixties counterculture. Indeed, the very language of "Be Here Now," cribbed from the work of Richard Alpert (aka Ram

Dass), an associate of Timothy Leary's at Harvard during the early days of LSD experimentation, is a case in point. Alpert's transformation into a leading guru of sixties counterculture forms an important narrative thread to the history of that era; his later work as an "out" gay man, working at the forefront of AIDS awareness and prison reform, among many other causes, is less well known. If there is indeed a "plurality of temporalities" to celebrate in the Woodstock story, part of that celebration involves the excavation of these alternative histories.

In telling this small slice of Elliot's story (his memoirs could be the basis for ten movies, from his sexual awakenings as a gay teen in fifties New York onward), we hope to simply let Woodstock happen, even as we witness and celebrate the extraordinary band of young visionaries and entrepreneurs who paused at the El Monaco on their way to Max's that summer. The entire story is infused with the "outside" joke that we never depict Elliot as ever getting to the concert himself; for our hero, as for us, the event itself remains just over the horizon.

Of course, the journey to Max's farm didn't just end with a weekend concert. For many of the team who produced Woodstock, that journey led them, just three-and-a-half months later, farther west, to Altamont, California, just north of San Francisco, where they went, as Mike Lang explains to Elliot in our film's final scene, to put on "a truly free concert," one that would feature the Rolling Stones— and the Hell's Angels. The spectacle of violence and death at Altamont has come, in retrospect, to mark "the end of the sixties," and, in the context of *Taking Woodstock*, a final reference to it could be taken as somehow "ironic," a knowing nod to the shattering of the Woodstock Nation's dreams. But perhaps we should understand Altamont (as well as the Manson Family's Tate and LaBianco murders, which occurred just prior to Woodstock) as themselves "causes" of the event we celebrate. It is not as if, in August 1969, an entire generation was innocent, and in December 1969, with Altamont and the arrest of the Manson Family, that innocence had ended; rather, Woodstock created, and continues to create, a kind of innocence that remains, in defiance of conventional temporality and causality, an immanent, potential, and productive force—long after the sixties ended.

Oh, and by the way, *Taking Woodstock* is a comedy!

—May 2009

TAKING WOODSTOCK

TAKING WOODSTOCK

by

James Schamus

Based on the book by

Elliot Tiber with Tom Monte

Official White: August 12, 2008
Blue Revision: September 3, 2008
Pink Revision: September 8, 2008

1   EXT. EL MONACO MOTEL - DAY   1

Summer, 1969. A Catskill dump. A single car in a weedy
parking lot. Needless to say, a prominent "Vacancy" sign out
front of the main building. A barn to one side with a ratty
handmade banner: "Home of the Earthlight Players." Clusters
of run-down cottages on the grounds, and a glimpse of swampy
White Lake at the bottom of the hill behind.

Jake Tiber, a tired-looking man in his sixties, is checking
the engine on his truck, parked on the front lawn. In faded
letters on the side of the truck: "Teichberg Roofing: Repairs
and Installation." Across the highway, a group of young
Jewish boys walks by, single file, on their way back to
POLONSKY'S BUNGALOWS AND SUMMER COLONY down the road. They
pause to stare at Jake. Jake looks back at them. They
silently move on.

A car pulls into the El Monaco's drive, and a rather
gentlemanly, fifty-ish man gets out. He hesitates before
entering the motel office.

2   INT. EL MONACO MOTEL - FRONT OFFICE -- DAY   2

The GENTLEMAN enters. Think Bates Motel, but Jewish. An array
of hand-painted signs (ABSOLUTELY NO REFUNDS, etc) and a mish-
mash of used furniture, a table with brochures hawking the
local attractions. Off to one side, a doorway opens onto a
makeshift bar and breakfast room.

                    GENTLEMAN
                 (British accent)
            Good morning? Hello?

Not a sign of life.

He peruses the brochures briefly.

                    GENTLEMAN (CONT'D)
            Hello? Anyone here?

A meaty hand pulls aside the curtain in the doorway behind
the desk, and Sonia emerges. Sonia is big, mid-sixties. She
breathes laboriously. Her small eyes regard the visitor with
suspicion, bordering -- indeed, spilling over into --
hostility.

                    SONIA
              (Russian Jewish accent)
            What is it?

> GENTLEMAN
> Good morning.

Silence.

> GENTLEMAN (CONT'D)
> I noticed the Vacancy sign out
> front.

> SONIA
> It said vacancy?

> GENTLEMAN
> Yes.

> SONIA
> So you come in without a
> reservation?

> GENTLEMAN
> Well, I was wondering if you did
> indeed have a room. Just for the
> night.

> SONIA
> This is a respectable
> establishment.

> GENTLEMAN
> Of course.

> SONIA
> You drove here?

> GENTLEMAN
> I've been touring the region, and
> return to New York city tomorrow.

> SONIA
> Is there a woman in your car?

> GENTLEMAN
> No - not that I know of!

She flips through an ancient and clearly purely decorative
ledger book. She keeps flipping through it, for a LONG time.

> SONIA
> I have a forest view single free.
> Number 17. Eight dollars. Cash.

The gentleman takes out his wallet, counts the eight dollars.
She re-counts it, turns to go.

                    GENTLEMAN
          Excuse me, the key?

She returns, fishes at random through a large shoe box filled
with all kinds of keys, selects one, and hands it to him.

                    SONIA
          Don't jump in the pool. The water
          we put in next week. For the
          summer.

With that, she returns to a back room, and he exits.

3   INT. EL MONACO MOTEL - BACK ROOM -- DAY   3

We hear the tv news as Sonia enters the room, puttering
around.

                    TV REPORTER (O.S.)
          There is no word yet as to whether
          President Nixon will make a stop-
          over in Saigon during his upcoming
          Asian trip, although officials here
          in the South Vietnamese capital are
          fervently hoping he will do so,
          giving them a much-needed show of
          support.

Sonia goes to the tv and changes the channel -- to a another
newscast.

She settles down heavily into a large frayed love seat
positioned in front of a television. Throughout, we stay in
extreme close up on her watchful face, hearing her breathing,
as the CREDITS commence and finish.

                    TV REPORTER 2 (O.S.)
          All along the Suez Canal, Israeli
          fighter jets have continued their
          sorties, hitting Egyptian artillery
          installations from Port Said to
          Port Suez. While there have been no
          indications of large-scale troop
          movements on either side of the
          border, nerves here are frayed, and
          it remains unclear what, if
          anything, the current moves
          signify.
                    (MORE)

                    TV REPORTER 2 (O.S.) (CONT'D)
          And after the commercial
          announcement, please stay tuned for
          our live reports from Houston and
          Florida as the Apollo 11 astronauts
          continue their flight through space
          -- destination, the moon.

Sonia keeps watching as a string of tv commercials launches.

As the credits end, we hear the bell on the office door ring
again. Sighing, Sonia lifts herself up and enters the front
office.

4   INT. EL MONACO MOTEL -- FRONT OFFICE -- DAY   4

The gentleman is back.

                    SONIA
          What?

                    GENTLEMAN
          Excuse me, but I can't possibly
          stay. This establishment isn't fit
          for human habitation.

                    SONIA
          Fine, go.

                    GENTLEMAN
          Yes, well, here is your key. It
          didn't fit the lock, but the door
          was open in any case.

                    SONIA
          You went into the room?

                    GENTLEMAN
          I did, yes. And now I must insist
          on you returning my eight dollars.

                    SONIA
          After you already used the room?
          What kind of scam are you running?
          And besides --

She gestures to the sign: No Refunds.

                    GENTLEMAN
          This is ridiculous. The so-called
          air conditioner was just an empty
          plastic box in the window.
                    (MORE)

                    GENTLEMAN (CONT'D)
          The room was filthy -- indeed, I
          discovered a small....hair....on
          the pillow...and there wasn't even
          a towel in the bathroom.

She points to another sign: TOWELS, ONE DOLLAR EXTRA.

                    GENTLEMAN (CONT'D)
          My Lord! And I attempted to use the
          phone to call you, but it was
          simply a handset, with a wire
          dangling from it, connected to
          nothing.

She points again: EXCUSE OUR APPEARANCE AS WE UPGRADE OUR
PHONE SYSTEM!

                    GENTLEMAN (CONT'D)
          But...but...

As he stammers, the door opens, and Sonia's son, Elliot, mid-
twenties, stands there, without entering.

                    ELLIOT
          Mom, please, we're late already.

                    SONIA
          My son, thank God you're here! This
          man is threatening me for a refund!

Elliot just sighs and leaves.

Sonia runs out after him. The gentleman stands there, at a
loss.

5   EXT. BETHEL BANK - DAY   5

        Bethel, New York. Sleepy would be one way to describe it.
        Depressed would be more accurate.

5A   The bank sits next to a gas station and across from a   5A
        tavern.

        We see Elliot, Sonia, and Jake walk from the roadway and into
        the bank.

6   INT. BETHEL BANK - DAY   6

        JACKSON SPIERS, branch manager, late-thirties, buttoned-up
        (though, this being 1969, the tie is loud and the lapels
        wide). He's not the happiest guy on earth.

                    JACKSON
          I'm sorry. You're over 5,000
          dollars in arrears on the mortgage.
          The home office is breathing down
          my neck --

Sitting across from him, the Teichberg clan. Sonia, her
husband, JAKE, put-upon, poor health, but still burly from
his years working as a roofer, and ELLIOT, who we notice now
is incongruously well-dressed for the appointment.

                    ELLIOT
          Mr. Spiers, the El Monaco Resort --

                    JACKSON
          -- It's a resort now?

                    ELLIOT
          ...and motel...is my parents'
          lifeblood. With the addition of the
          swimming pool, and these new town-
          wide marketing initiatives --

                    JACKSON
          Initiatives?

                    ELLIOT
          As you know, I have been elected
          the President of the Bethel Chamber
          of Commerce --

                    SONIA
          -- the youngest president in their
          history!

                    ELLIOT
              (talking too fast)
          We've decided to erect a tourist
          information booth, right off 17B,
          in fact, and I have agreed on
          behalf of the El Monaco to lease at
          no cost some road frontage to the
          endeavor, which should
          coincidentally drive heavy tourist
          traffic right to our door. In
          addition --

                    JACKSON
          Please, Elliot, you know I do
          everything I can to help. We even
          bought one of your paintings...

We see a pleasant abstract landscape, its modernist aesthetic out of place in the bank's otherwise down-home ambience, on the wall.

                    JACKSON (CONT'D)
          ...But don't try to sell me on
          those...those singles weekends, or
          that culture festival or whatever
          schemes were supposed to dig you
          out last summer --

                    ELLIOT
          -- We're going to go classical with
          the festival this year, maybe a
          string quartet, but contemporary,
          like Morton Feldman? Very cutting
          edge. And we've got a theater
          troupe in the barn.

                    JACKSON
          You have a theater troupe in the
          barn?

                    ELLIOT
          The Earthlight Players. Vassar
          graduates, some of them.

                    JACKSON
          They live in the barn?

                    ELLIOT
          They do everything in the barn. You
          haven't seen the sign?

                    JACKSON
          What sign?

                    ELLIOT
          The sign in front of the barn.

                    SONIA
          Mr. Spiers, My God, please! We come
          here, begging, begging for mercy,
          but what do you give us? This
          fixation about the barn! What is it
          with you and the barn?

                    JACKSON
          I was just --

                    SONIA
           -- I'm an old woman Mr. Spiers,
          I've suffered.
                    (MORE)

                    SONIA (CONT'D)
        I walked here all the way from
        Minsk in Russia in twenty-foot snow
        drifts, a thousand miles across
        Siberia, I escaped the pogroms, the
        Tsar's secret police, with nothing
        but cold potatoes in my pockets --

                    JACKSON
              (he's heard this spiel
              before)
        Mrs. Teichberg, please --

                    SONIA
        And for what? More persecution!
        It's because we're Jewish, I know
        it, isn't it --

                    JACKSON
        Mrs. Teichberg, please, this is the
        Catskills, half the summer colonies
        are Jewish, they're all our
        clients!

                    SONIA
              (standing)
        Until the day they need you -- and
        then on goes the gas!

                    ELLIOT
        Mom, calm down! Jackson, just --
        just give us a couple of months.
        The summer season is coming up, and
        I honestly do have some real money
        owed me from my interior design
        business in the city. Please?

7   EXT. EL MONACO MOTEL -- DAY   7

The Teichbergs walk back along the road, glum.

As they pass by the Polonsky cottage colony across the
street, we hear the megaphone announcements indicating the
activities at the thriving motel:

                    ANNOUNCER
              (Jewish accent)
        Kinder-dance class begins in ten
        minutes. Mother-son ballroom class
        will start immediately after at 11.
        That's kinder-dancing for the
        kiddies in ten minutes.

8   EXT. EL MONACO MOTEL -- FRONT OFFICE -- DAY   8

Sonia huffs her way into the back room.

Elliot stays back with his father.

> ELLIOT
> Dad, you gotta get Ma to lay off
> the Nazi stuff and let me handle
> this.

> JAKE
> You think I can tell your mother
> what to do?

Elliot knows he's right.

> ELLIOT
> I gotta get back to the city. I'll
> see you Friday. (pause) We'll get
> the money.

> JAKE
> Let them take this miserable dump.
> I'll die in peace, in Florida.

9   EXT. HIGHWAY -- DAY   9

Elliot drives his car back to New York, listening to the
radio. Sign says "NY Thruway, New York City 87 miles."

10   EXT. MONTAGE -- DAY   10

The music playing in Elliot's car rises, and accompanies
split screen images of the Catskills in the sixties: Jewish
summer colonies, fishing outings, the local racetrack, etc.

11   EXT. ELLIOT'S APARTMENT BUILDING -- DAY   11

Elliot finds a parking spot near the front of the building.
He gets out of his car, pauses before he enters.

12   OMITTED   12

13   OMITTED   13

14 INT. LOBBY -- ELLIOT'S APARTMENT BUILDING -- DAY 14

Elliot enters and heads for the elevator.

The doorman nods, a bit snobbily.

>   DOORMAN
> Mr. Tiber.

>   ELLIOT
> George.

>   DOORMAN
> I admitted your sister some time
> ago.

>   ELLIOT
> Thanks.

>   DOORMAN
> And some gentlemen from Van's.

>   ELLIOT
> Oh. Yeah.

Elliot enters the elevator.

15 INT. ELLIOT'S APARTMENT -- DAY 15

Elliot walks in. Workmen are wrapping up furniture and
stacking boxes. ESTHER, late thirties, calls out to him.

>   ESTHER
> There you are!

>   ELLIOT
> Hey sis.

>   ESTHER
> How did it go at the bank?

>   ELLIOT
> How do you think it went? Til the
> end of summer, and that's it.

>   ESTHER
> And what about the money those
> mobsters owe you -- for that
> nightclub you designed?

                  ELLIOT
They have a surprisingly strict
policy about paying designers. They
don't.

She lets it sink in.

He walks over to a stack of oil paintings leaning against one
of the walls and lifts one up, a beautiful abstract canvas.

                  ELLIOT (CONT'D)
You want some more paintings?

                  ESTHER
I already have ten of them. And you
know Joe hates them. But thanks.

He puts it back.

                  ESTHER (CONT'D)
Elliot, this is a big mistake.

                  ELLIOT
I never could afford to live here
anyhow. And now it's official. I'm
broke.

                  ESTHER
Of course you are, after all the
money you've sunk into that hell
hole of theirs. And I bet Ma's
never even said a word of thanks,
has she?

                  ELLIOT
No...but I can sense it -- the
special way she sometimes looks at
me with just her left eye.

He's about to take a seat when one of the moving men grabs
the chair and walks out with it. He sits on the floor.

                  ESTHER
Oh Elliot. Now's your time, to go
to California like you've always
wanted, to paint and design, be
free, not a slave for those two in
that Catskill prison.

                  ELLIOT
I can't give up on them now.

ESTHER
Why not? They gave up on you a long
time ago.

ELLIOT
No, they didn't. It's the opposite.
I'm the one they still want around.
I guess that means they love me
more than you.

ESTHER
That must be a great consolation to
you.

ELLIOT
How'd you do it sis? How'd you get
so sane?

ESTHER
(getting up to go, gives
him a kiss on the
forehead)
I just walked, Elliot. I just
walked away until I found a place
of my own.

16   INT. GAY BAR -- NIGHT   16

The place is packed with a varied mix of New York's gay
underground, tilting heavily to the leather end, newly
energized after the recent Stonewall riots.

We find Elliot at the bar with his friend Steven.

STEVEN
Don't look now, but that
photographer guy, in the black
leather pants, he's staring at your
ass.

A quick shot reveals Robert Mapplethorpe staring at them from
across the room.

ELLIOT
Him? I don't have the energy
tonight.

STEVEN
Oh, c'mon, you could use a good
whipping. It'll pick you right up.

                    ELLIOT
What I could use is five thousand
dollars. That'd pick me up -
straight to San Francisco.

                    STEVEN
I was thinking, why don't you just
turn that motel into a gay resort.
Wouldn't that be amazing? Put your
mom into a kind of bondage leather
thing, give her a whip in one hand,
a stack of potato pancakes in the
other.

                    ELLIOT
        (almost to himself)
My dad makes the pancakes. Mom
makes the cholent. Her cholent's
good. You can cement bricks with
it. If you paste it in your hair,
it forms a concrete helmet. The
helmet will protect you from the
baseball bats crashing down on your
head by the local John Birchers,
some of whom are also trying to get
into your pants, because hey, what
would small town life be without
the hypocrisy on top of the
intolerance? Yeah, so why go to
Fire Island when the El Monaco
International Resort awaits?

                    STEVEN
Wow, Elliot. So glad I was able to
cheer you up. C'mon, let's dance.

                    ELLIOT
You dance, Steven. I'll drink.

Steven goes off -- we see Mapplethorpe continuing to stare at
Elliot.

17   EXT. GAY BAR -- NIGHT   17

Elliot exits, breathes in the early summer air. He hears a
small commotion down the street -- three cops have a drag
queen spread-eagled against a patrol car; one holds her down
with his night stick while another frisks her.

                    COP
        (to Elliot)
You want something?

Elliot turns in the other direction, walks into the night.

18 EXT. EL MONACO MOTEL -- POOL -- DAY 18

A beautiful early summer day. Elliot is filling the pool.

Jake lugs over some bottles of Clorox, pours one in.

>   ELLIOT
> Dad. That's bleach, for laundry.

>   JAKE
> It kills the germs. What's the
> difference?

19 INT. EL MONACO MOTEL -- COTTAGE -- DAY 19

Elliot, hard at work, scrubbing a toilet.

Bucket in hand, he goes back into the motel room. Strips the
bed. Walks outside. His mother passes by.

>   SONIA
> What, Elli? What are you doing with
> those sheets?!

>   ELLIOT
> They're dirty.

>   SONIA
> Let me see!

She takes them, sniffs them.

>   SONIA (CONT'D)
> Nothing. Those two, they didn't do
> nothing in there. Shake them, put
> them back.

>   ELLIOT
> But ma!

>   SONIA
> Electricity, detergent, whose
> paying for all that? Stupid boy!

She goes on her way, and spots across the lawn a lone young
woman spinning and dancing in front of the barn.

                         SONIA (CONT'D)
                    And you, theater girl -- get back
                    in the barn!

The girl looks up at her, runs back into the barn.

20   INT. BETHEL CHURCH BASEMENT -- EVENING   20

A meeting in progress. Elliot and five or six of the locals.
He bangs a gavel.

                         ELLIOT
                    Let's call to order. C'mon
                    everyone. Are the minutes from last
                    meeting approved?

Annie, 70s, sweet, raises her hand.

                         ANNIE
                    I thought the minutes were lovely.

                         ELLIOT
                    Thank you Annie.

                         ANNIE
                    And I'm not just saying that.

                         ELLIOT
                    Thank you.

                         ANNIE
                    You're welcome.

                         ELLIOT
                    So. Any new business.

                         FRANK
                    Not much in these parts!

A polite giggle from the room.

                         ELLIOT
                    Ok, Frank. We all said last meeting
                    we'd each bring some new ideas to
                    the table.

                         FRANK
                    Well, ok. We've got a lot of dairy
                    farms around here, right? And a
                    fair number of bulls.
                              (MORE)

                    FRANK (CONT'D)
          Ok, you've all heard of the running
          of the bulls, in that town in
          Spain, Pampoona --

                    ELLIOT
          --Pamplona --

                    FRANK
          Ok, Pamplona. Well, no one's doing
          one in the Catskills. Seems to be a
          big draw over there.

Silence.

                    ANNIE
          It would be very amusing to see all
          those Jews from Levitsky's summer
          colony, you know, the ones with the
          black top hats and the curls,
          running for their lives chased by
          our local livestock. Wouldn't that
          be a wonderful sight!

                    ELLIOT
          I'm writing it all down. Any other
          ideas?

                    MARGARET
          What about the monorail?

                    FRANK
          Marge, you can't bring that up
          every meeting.

                    MARGARET
          I've written to the governor, but I
          think a letter from the entire
          Chamber of Commerce would be much
          more effective. A monorail,
          directly connecting downtown New
          York with White Lake, would be a
          tremendous spur to the local
          economy. You see, if there were
          black-out shades on the windows of
          the monorail, the travellers would
          depart the city and arrive in the
          country. The sight upon their
          arrival would be especially
          dramatic!

                    DAN
               (no-nonsense, mid-
               thirties, sitting with
               his wife Carol)
                    (MORE)

                    DAN (CONT'D)
          Jesus. Look people, I said I'd come
          back to these meetings if you could
          stay out of la-la-land for just
          once. We've got serious local
          issues, and serious business to do.

                    MARGARET
          Such as?

                    DAN
          For starters, I need a permit to
          use the town landing for the fish-
          toss tournament next month.

                    MARGARET
          I knew it. Just here for your own
          purposes.

                    ELLIOT
               (opening a small change
                box)
          Now, Marge, c'mon. Let's see the
          application.

Dan hands it over.

                    ELLIOT (CONT'D)
          All in order. One dollar.

Dan gives him the dollar.

                    ELLIOT (CONT'D)
          And I've got my application for our
          annual El Monaco summer music and
          art event, which will also
          inaugurate the first season of our
          tourist information kiosk. Annie,
          if your grandson and his friends
          want to play again this year, he
          should give me a call.

Elliot takes out his own dollar bill.

                    ELLIOT (CONT'D)
          Do I hear a motion to approve these
          permits?

                    ANNIE
          I so move.

                    ELLIOT
          Seconded?

                              DAN
                    For crying out loud, ok, seconded.

Elliot stamps the permits.

21   EXT. BETHEL CHURCH PARKING LOT -- EVENING   21

Everyone from the meeting saying their farewells.

Dan and Carol pause by their convertible, parked next to
Elliot's car.

                              CAROL
                    'Night, Elliot.

                              ELLIOT
                    Good night, Carol.

As Elliot is about to get into his car, he's jolted by the
sudden screaming of BILLY, who has apparently been sleeping
in the back seat of his brother Dan's convertible and now
jumps up.

                              BILLY
                    Fuck! Fuck! Take him down,
                    motherfuckers!

                              ELLIOT
                    Jesus!

We now get a look at Billy. Dirty army jacket, long tangled
hair -- your basic post-trauma Vietnam Vet. Billy wakens from
his flashback, a look of confusion on his face.

                              BILLY
                    What?

                              DAN
                    For fuck's sake, Billy. Get back in
                    the car.

                              ELLIOT
                    Hey Billy, you're back. That's
                    great.

                              BILLY
                    Yeah. Stayin' with big brother Dan
                    and his beautiful wife Carol here
                    til I get my own pad.

                    DAN
          Yeah. Cause little brother Billy
          made a tiny little pit stop in
          Bangkok and blew all his army pay,
          didn't he, Billy?

                    BILLY
          Shit, man. Bangkok! Fuckin'
          Bangkok!

                    DAN
          We gotta go.

                    ELLIOT
          Great seeing you back home, Billy.

Dan and Carol quickly get into the car. He turns the engine
and they pull away as Elliot watches them.

22   EXT. EL MONACO MOTEL -- BUNGALOW BY THE LAKE -- NIGHT   22

To establish. We see part of a car parked discreetly behind
the bungalow, out of sight.

23   INT. EL MONACO MOTEL -- BUNGALOW BY THE LAKE -- NIGHT   23

In the dark room, we barely make out two intertwined bodies,
the sound of some pretty rough sex, ending in someone's
climax.

A pause. Someone flips the light on, and we discover Elliot
and Dan in bed. Dan immediately hops up and starts to get
dressed. Elliot watches him from the bed.

                    ELLIOT
          Just a pit stop tonight?

                    DAN
          I can't leave Carol alone with that
          brother of mine for more than an
          hour. He gives her the creeps.

                    ELLIOT
          He'll get better. I guess he's just
          upset about shooting people, and
          people shooting him, and stuff like
          that...

                    DAN
          He's a fuckin' nightmare. Comes
          back looking like a hippie and
          smelling like one too.

                    ELLIOT
          What do hippies smell like?

                    DAN
          And I swear to god, he's become a
          fuckin' commie. I kid you not. The
          crap that comes out of his mouth.
          No respect for persons or property.
          None at all. No values. It's
          disgusting.

                    ELLIOT
          Well, it's good of you and Carol to
          take him in.

Dan's demeanor softens.

                    DAN
          Yeah. (shakes his head) Billy. Hey,
          you wouldn't have any work for him
          around here?

                    ELLIOT
          If we could afford it, sure.

                    DAN
             (nodding)
          Yeah. Plus, wouldn't want him
          catching me coming over here.

Finished dressing, Don walks out without another word. Elliot
watches the door close behind him.

                    ELLIOT
             (muttering)
          I love you too.

24   OMITTED   24

25   EXT. SLATTERY'S DRUG STORE -- DAY   25

      Elliot drives up as Jackson, from the bank, is walking out.

                    JACKSON
          Elliot.

                         ELLIOT
              Hi Jackson.

                         JACKSON
              I saw the notice in the paper,
              about the theater company. Chekhov
              [he pronounces it "check-off"]. Two
              sisters.

                         ELLIOT
              Three Sisters.

                         JACKSON
              That's a lot of sisters...

                         ELLIOT
              More than one or two...

                         JACKSON
              Yeah, three. Should be quite a
              show.

                         ELLIOT
              Yeah. You think anyone will come?

                         JACKSON
              No.

Elliot just nods.

                         JACKSON (CONT'D)
              Honestly Elliot, why do you bother?

26   INT. SLATTERY'S DRUG STORE -- DAY   26

An old-fashioned counter coffee shop.

Elliot takes a seat at the counter.

                         DAVE
              The usual?

                         ELLIOT
              Extra bacon, please.

                         DAVE
              You got it.

A couple of other regulars acknowledge Elliot. One of them, a
kindly, thin dairy farmer, is paying his check.

                    MAX
          Hey Elliot, I hear you've moved up
          here permanently.

                    ELLIOT
          Just helping mom and dad for the
          season.

                    MAX
          I hope you have another one of
          those festivals. Miriam and I love
          listening to your records out on
          that lawn.

                    ELLIOT
          Sure Max. And this year I'm going
          to try to get a live quartet.

                    BOB
             (holding up the local
              paper)
          Looks like you're gonna have some
          competition.

                    DAVE
          What, there's a recall vote at the
          Chamber of Commerce?

                    BOB
          Says here that Wallkill's gonna
          have a music festival, too, some
          hippie thing got thrown outta
          Woodstock so they've set themselves
          up in Wallkill.

                    ELLIOT
             (taking the paper)
          Wow, Janis Joplin.

                    BOB
          Guess that beats playing a bunch of
          records on your lawn. (getting up
          to leave) Then again, it'll
          probably be some kind of antiwar
          riot. Let Wallkill have 'em.

Dave puts a huge breakfast plate in front of Elliot.

                    DAVE
          Extra bacon.

27   INT. EL MONACO MOTEL -- MOTEL ROOM -- DAY   27

Elliot cleaning again.

He's about to change the sheets on the bed, but instead leans over, sniffs them, folds them back.

He lies down on the bed, looks up at the ceiling.

(Over music, another brief montage)

27A   EXT. EL MONACO MOTEL -- DAY   27A

Jake lifting supplies out of the back of his truck; he pauses, winded and aching;

27B   INT. EL MONACO MOTEL -- KITCHEN -- DAY   27B

Sonia in the kitchen stirring a pot of beans.

27C   (Split screen: tv images, Rowan and Martin's Laugh-In,   27C
antiwar protests, Vietnam, the Andy Griffith show.)

28   INT. EL MONACO MOTEL -- BAR AREA -- NIGHT   28

Elliot is cleaning up. Jake behind the bar, pouring himself a drink.

Elliot stops what he's doing, looks at his father disapprovingly.

                    JAKE
           If your mother comes in, I'm not
           drinking.

                    ELLIOT
           You are drinking, whether she comes
           in or not.

                    JAKE
           It's just one -- and stay out of my
           business.

As he lifts the glass, he winces in pain.

                    ELLIOT
           Shoulder?

                    JAKE
          Yeah.

                    ELLIOT
          I thought it was the hip.

                    JAKE
          It is the hip -- and the shoulder.

They sit in silence for a minute.

                    ELLIOT
          Dad?

                    JAKE
          What?

                    ELLIOT
          I was thinking, maybe we're going
          to have a fire.

Pause.

                    JAKE
          What's the point? I stopped paying
          the insurance.

                    ELLIOT
          Ah, right, hadn't thought of that.
          How about we get insurance. Then
          maybe we could have a fire, like
          the Malansky's.

Another pause.

                    JAKE
          We're so spread out here. Too many
          buildings for the old Jewish
          lightning.

                    ELLIOT
          Hmmm. You're right. Ok, no fire. It
          didn't feel right anyway.

Jake gets off his stool, shuffles to the door.

                    ELLIOT (CONT'D)
          So, Pop. You thought this through
          already, didn't you?

Without a word, Jake walks out of the bar, leaving Elliot
alone in the dark space.

29   EXT. EL MONACO MOTEL -- NIGHT   29

       To establish. An early summer night. Elliot walks to the
       barn.

30   INT./EXT. EL MONACO BARN -- NIGHT   30

       The small group of players is rehearsing an avant-garde
       version of Three Sisters. Three of the players are stage
       front, declaiming.

                         MALE PLAYER
                 This liquor is made from beetles!

                         FEMALE PLAYER
                 No! No! That's horrible!

                         FEMALE PLAYER 2
                 Tonight's dinner will be roast
                 turkey - and for dessert, an apple
                 tart!

       Behind them, the rest of the ensemble stands in line,
       responding to each line with exhalations of percussive moans
       in unison.

                         DEVON
                     (smashing a prop clock on
                      the stage floor)
                 Ha, I killed it!

                         FEMALE PLAYER 2
                 That clock was our mother's!

                         DEVON
                 Your mother! Your mother! But maybe
                 I didn't break it! Maybe it only
                 looks like I broke it! Maybe we
                 only think we exist when we really
                 don't!

       DEVON, the company's leader, sees Elliot walk in carrying a
       battered music case. Devon steps toward Elliot, indicating to
       the group that they should continue their rehearsing.

       Elliot puts the music case on a chair and opens it for Devon,
       who reaches down and takes out an oboe. They talk quietly.

                         DEVON (CONT'D)
                 Thanks Elliot.

                    ELLIOT
          It hasn't been touched since my
          glory days in the Midwood High
          School band. How's the show shaping
          up.

                    DEVON
          We're really getting into it.

                    ELLIOT
          Great. I just hope you guys are
          prepared -- you're probably going
          to outnumber the audience.

                    DEVON
          It only takes one extra soul to
          make it theater, man. And theater
          is transformation. But it's hard.
          Concentrating...

                    ELLIOT
          Concentrating...On?

                    DEVON
          We're just, I don't know, hungry,
          man.

                    ELLIOT
          Hungry as in --

                    DEVON
          Yeah, as in hungry, for foodstuffs.
          You don't have some potatoes or
          sunflower seeds or anything. I
          could barter some very special
          grass.

                    ELLIOT
          Uh, me and grass, you don't want to
          know. But let me see what I can
          steal from my mom and you can pay
          us back after the first show -- or
          not, I guess.

                    DEVON
          Front row seats, man. On the house,
          for you!

Behind them, the players continue to declaim:

                    FEMALE PLAYER
          I'm bored! I'm bored! I'm bored!
          The house is ours, not his.
                         (MORE)

                    FEMALE PLAYER (CONT'D)
          But he took out that mortgage, and
          now his wife has all the money!

                    FEMALE PLAYER 2
          He just plays on his fiddle and
          does nothing! I can't take it any
          longer! I can't! I can't! Please
          throw me out, just throw me out! I
          can't take it!

31   INT. EL MONACO MOTEL -- FRONT OFFICE -- NIGHT   31

     Elliot, working on the account book, when the phone rings.

                    ELLIOT
          Hello?

     We hear the voice of his friend Steven on the other line.

                    STEVEN (O.S.)
          Hey Elliot!

                    ELLIOT
          Steven! What are you doing calling
          long distance?

                    STEVEN (O.S.)
          I just made bail -- the pigs raided
          the bar again, can you believe it?
          Come back, I think we're going to
          have another riot!

                    ELLIOT
          Come up here. You can start a riot
          here in White Lake.

                    STEVEN (O.S.)
          Wild....I was just calling, you
          know, New York hasn't been as much
          fun without you -- I mean, it
          hasn't been as depressing, but you
          know, in a fun way. So me and
          Marcus, we're hitching a ride with
          that art dealer, remember him?

                    ELLIOT
          The one with the doll collection?

                    STEVEN (O.S.)
          Yeah. We're moving to San
          Francisco, man! You wanna join?

Elliot doesn't know what to say. He holds the phone for a moment against his shoulder, looks out the screen door at the peaceful, dark night outside.

>   STEVEN (CONT'D)
>   Elliot? You there?

>   ELLIOT
>   Yeah, I'm still here. Hey, thanks
>   for the call. It's good to hear
>   your voice. And drop me a line when
>   you get there, ok?

32   INT. EL MONACO MOTEL -- BAR -- DAY   32

Elliot is busy making more signs:

"Presidential Suite" "Swimming Pool: Surf at Your own Risk"

>   SONIA
>   Elli! There's something moving in
>   the bushes!

33   EXT. WOODY SWAMP -- DAY   33

Elliot walks through the woods toward the swamp.

He sees a rustling in the bushes.

Gingerly, he approaches.

Suddenly, Billy, in full camouflage, jumps out.

>   ELLIOT
>   Holy shit! Billy!

>   BILLY
>   Take cover, man!

>   ELLIOT
>   What?

Billy comes out of it, slightly.

>   ELLIOT (CONT'D)
>   Billy. What is it?

                      BILLY
We're surrounded man. Can't you
feel it? It's like, when the radio
was busted, and we fragged that
fuckin' sergeant, so then they
just leave us out here, but
someone's gotta go back and call in
air support, cause I gotta stay
with O'Connor -- he doesn't have
any feet, man!

Billy sits on the grass. Closes his eyes.

Elliot sits next to him.

                      ELLIOT
It's ok, Billy. Umm. The radio's
working in the office. I can call
from there...And you can, um, cover
me...Right? I'll, uh, take a squad,
and, uh, do some recon, and the VC
will never see me, and then I'll
call in the coordinates, and, uh...

Billy opens his yes, looks at Elliot.

                      BILLY
What the fuck are you talking
about, Elliot?

                      ELLIOT
I don't know. I thought maybe I
could be in your flashback or
something. If it made you feel
better.

                      BILLY
          (gives Elliot a look)
That's cool.

Billy takes a few breaths, pulls out a joint, lights it.

                 BILLY (CONT'D)
Man, I really am fucked up... You
think I should take the pills they
gave me, at the V.A.? I should
probably take those fuckin' pills,
but then I just sleep all the time,
and then there's the fuckin'
nightmares. Fuck.

He offers Elliot the joint. Elliot declines.

                    BILLY (CONT'D)
          Never thought I'd end up back here.

                    ELLIOT
          Me neither.

                    BILLY
          I'm thinking, maybe I should do
          another tour.

                    ELLIOT
          That doesn't sound like such a good
          idea.

                    BILLY
          Over in 'Nam, I'm fuckin' normal,
          you know what I'm saying? Hey. You
          should join up.

                    ELLIOT
          Me? They wouldn't let me if I
          wanted.

                    BILLY
          Yeah?

                    ELLIOT
          ...Flat feet...

                    BILLY
          ...Riiiggghht. Feet. Fuck. You're
          not fuckin' normal, Elliot.

Elliot gets up, helps Billy up.

                    ELLIOT
          I guess not.

                    BILLY
          Man. All I know is, we're fuckin'
          surrounded here.

                    ELLIOT
          You can say that again!

34   INT. EL MONACO MOTEL -- FRONT OFFICE -- DAY   34

     Elliot sinks back down at the front desk chair. Sonia comes
     in with a plate of food and plops it down in front of him.

                    SONIA
          Eat.

She goes back to the bar.

He sighs, glancing at the place. He leans over and picks up the newspaper:

> "Wallkill Pulls Permit on Music
> Festival
> Mayor: 'Hippies Not Welcome Here'"

A couple of the Earthlight Theater Troupe members come in.

>   DEVON
>   Hey, thanks Elliot for painting
>   that backdrop -- everyone loves the
>   colors, man. It's like a mandala,
>   except, um, it's not really like a
>   mandala, with the colors....More
>   like, ah, M and Ms...

>   ELLIOT
>   You're welcome Dev.

Elliot looks at his plate of food.

>   ELLIOT (CONT'D)
>   Hey, you guys want some? Cholent.

They look down at the plate, catching a whiff, trading glances.

>   DEVON
>   Uh, hmmm, maybe next time.

>   MALE PLAYER
>   Yeah, I'm cool.

Devon sees the headline.

>   DEVON
>   Hey man, what's up with that?

>   ELLIOT
>   (picks up the paper,
>   reading)
>   The festival. Yeah, the locals
>   killed it.

>   DEVON
>   In Wallkill.

>   MALE PLAYER
>   The Wallkillians killed it.

                    DEVON
          Bummer. We were all hoping to score
          some tickets and go over for it.
          Could of been beautiful. Joan Baez,
          Grateful Dead, The Who.

                    MALE PLAYER
          Maybe even Dylan.

                    DEVON
          Dylan, yeah.

Elliot pauses, thinking, then opens the desk drawer and
starts riffling through stacks of paper and bills.

                    MALE PLAYER
          Yeah, Dylan.

                    DEVON
          Yeah...Dylan.

Elliot doesn't seem to be listening as he keeps looking
through the papers in the desk.

                    DEVON (CONT'D)
          You all right there, Elliot?

Elliot finally finds what he's looking for, and picks up the
phone.

                    ELLIOT
               (into the phone)
          Hi, Alice. I need you to connect me
          to something called Woodstock
          Ventures in New York City, a
          gentleman there by the name
          of...(looks at the paper) Michael
          Lang.

Elliot looks up at Devon.

                    ELLIOT (CONT'D)
          They lost their permit, right?

He holds up the permit for his own music festival in his
hand.

                    DEVON
               (suddenly excited)
          Far fuckin' out, Elliot! They
          should all come here to the barn,
          man! And put on a show with you and
          us! We got the space, right?
               (MORE)

                    DEVON (CONT'D)
          And you could put everyone up here
          at the El Monaco. That'd be truly
          beautiful!

                    MALE PLAYER
          Dylan...in the barn!

WE HEAR A VOICE IN THE PHONE AS ELLIOT PUTS IT TO HIS EAR,
SHUSHING THEM.

                    SECRETARY (O.S.)
          Woodstock Ventures.

35   EXT. EL MONACO MOTEL -- DAY   35

Elliot is laying out sheets on the front lawn, making the
sign of a cross with them. His mother rushes over, Jake not
far behind.

                    SONIA
          Elli! Elli! What is this with the
          sheets?

                    ELLIOT
          What does it look like? I'm making
          a big cross on the lawn.

                    SONIA
          With the clean sheets! Jake, our
          boy's gone crazy! Making a Ku Klux
          Klan rally on our property!

                    ELLIOT
          No, it's so they can find us.

                    SONIA
          Who?

Just then, a whirring sound can be heard approaching from
over the lake, and above them appears an old, decommissioned
army helicopter. From across the lawn, the doors to the barn
burst open and the members of the Earthlight Players spill
out. They begin to dance around the white sheets, some of
them disrobing, as the helicopter descends. Sonia is
practically screaming as she backs towards the motel office.

The helicopter lands, it's whirring blades slowing down, as
everyone pauses to await the discharge its passengers.

The door flings open, and out jumps Michael, fringe vest, no
shirt, jeans, and sandals, grinning.

The theatre troupe let out a cheer. Following Michael are an
assistant, Tisha, and two hip but serious looking men, Mel
and Stan.

Michael walks up to Elliot, looks him over quickly and
extends his hand.

                    MICHAEL
          Hey man. Good to see you.

They shake.

                    MICHAEL (CONT'D)
          You don't remember me, Elli?

                    ELLIOT
          Do we know each other?

                    MICHAEL
          Bensonhurst! Seventy-third Street.
          I lived down the street from you
          man. We played stickball. I'm
          Michael Lang, you're Elli
          Tiechberg.

                    ELLIOT
          Wow. I kind of remem --

Michael turns to Elliot's parents.

                    MICHAEL
          Mrs. Tiechberg! Hey, it's Michael,
          from the neighborhood.

He gives her a big hug and kiss. She acts like she's been
embraced by a martian. Over his shoulder, she now notices the
theater troupe.

                    SONIA
          Excuse me. (to the troupe) You!
          Cover your parts! We have company!
          Shoo!

They scatter.

                    MICHAEL
          Far out. So. Here we are.

                    ELLIOT
          Right. Yes, as I mentioned on the
          phone --

                         MICHAEL
               You have a permit. That's very
               cool, Elli.

Elliot fishes the permit from his pocket, unfolds it, and
hands it to Michael. The two other men gather round Michael
as he reads it. A fearful silence for Elliot as he watches
them. Michael nods to them men; they nod back.

                         MEL
               It's a start.

                         MICHAEL
                    (smiling)
               Very cool.

Two stretch limos now pull up into the parking lot, and a
small army of Woodstock people emerge to join them, a local
real estate agent.

                         MICHAEL (CONT'D)
                    (smiling)
               Hey people! Welcome to Elliot's
               place. Hey, Elli, can we take a
               look around?

                         ELLIOT
               Of course. I'll show you the whole
               place.

36   EXT. EL MONACO MOTEL -- DAY   36

We follow the group as it makes its way through the various
cabin clusters. People silently note Elliot's signage:
"Presidential Wing, formerly the Moulin Rouge Wing." "Marilyn
Monroe Pool House and Cabana Club. Invited Guests Only. All
Others will be Incarcerated Pending $5 Payment to Sonia the
Pool Savant."

                         MICHAEL
               And you've got some open land here,
               right?

                         ELLIOT
               Absolutely, just up here and down
               towards the lake.

37   EXT. EL MONACO MOTEL -- SWAMP -- DAY   37

Cut to the group slugging through a marshy scrub forest,
their feet sinking in the mud.

They pass a sign: "Coming Soon on this Site: 200-Story
Convention Center, Gambling Casino and Health Spa -- Parking
for 2,000"

Mel turns to Michael.

> MEL
> Michael, for Christ's sake, it's a
> swamp.

Michael sees the looming defeat in Elliot's eyes.

> MICHAEL
> Maybe we could get some bulldozers
> in here and level it, right?

> STAN
> You're kidding me.

> MICHAEL
> (sotto voce)
> He owns it. He's got a permit. He's
> the president of the Chamber of
> Commerce.

> STAN
> And because of that you're going to
> drown thousands of kids in a swamp?

> ELLIOT
> (overhearing,
> halfheartedly)
> Look, honestly, you guys can do
> whatever you want to here. That's
> fine with us, really. You could,
> for example, you could detonate an
> incredible amount of explosives and
> it would dry everything out
> immediately, and then you could
> just compact the ashes down and
> people could sit on that...you
> know...?

> MICHAEL
> Radical thinking Elliot. I like it.

> MEL
> I assume you've got a permit for
> that too?

                         ELLIOT
                Or, ok, we get some big cranes and
                hang like a giant parachute over
                the fields here, and everyone could
                sit on it...No? Or how about you
                just nuke the whole place....

The group is walking back already.

                         MICHAEL
                Hey. Don't lose that creativity,
                man.

                         ELLIOT
                     (defeated)
                Yeah.

They trudge back to the parking area and front lawn.

37A   EXT. MOTEL - FRONT LAWN AREA - DAY   37A

At the motel, Sonia is waiting for them, clearly impressed by
the limos and the helicopter.

                         SONIA
                Elli, have you offered
                accommodation to everyone? We may
                not have vacancy for everyone, as
                the season is starting, but of
                course --

                         ELLIOT
                Ma, they're not staying.

                         SONIA
                Stay! Stay! Look, my husband is
                bringing refreshments.

And indeed, Jake is lugging a box with some drinks in it, but
most of the group is already heading back to the cars, not
paying attention.

                         MICHAEL
                Thank you Mrs. Teichberg.

                         SONIA
                Here. Try some of this, the best
                chocolate milk in New York. Made
                just down the road.

She hands him a box of Yasgur's Fresh Chocolate Milk.

                    MICHAEL
              (taking a sip to be
              polite)
          Wow. That is excellent chocolate
          milk, Mrs. Teichberg.

                    ELLIOT
              (lightbulb going off)
          It comes from local cows.

                    MICHAEL
          Far out.

                    ELLIOT
          They eat local grass.

                    MICHAEL
          That must be some healthy grass.

                    ELLIOT
          And there's a lot of it, in big
          fields, just a few miles down the
          road from us.

                    MICHAEL
          I'm catching your drift Elli!

                    ELLIOT
              (running back to the
              office)
          Let me get my keys.

     Elliot runs into the motel.

38   EXT. YASGUR'S FARM -- FIELD -- DAY   38

     Max Yasgur, Elliot, Michael, Mel, Stan, Tisha and the group
     stand atop a hill overlooking a beautiful, pastoral landscape
     -- sloping hills descend to form a perfect amphitheater. The
     Woodstock folks are quietly elated.

                    MAX
              (to Michael)
          I've always been a big supporter of
          Elliot here in Bethel, and I always
          enjoy his music festival every
          summer.

                    MICHAEL
          That's why we're here.

     Michael looks out over the field, almost in a trance.

                    MICHAEL (CONT'D)
               (almost to himself)
          It's fate. It's beautiful.

                    MAX
          Miriam and I donate the yogurt and
          milk.

                    MIRIAM
          Although some of the local young
          people, the music they play, it can
          be a little trying, if you know
          what I mean. It sometimes seems
          they actually like to stand with
          their electric guitars quite close
          to those amplifying speakers -- as
          if on purpose -- to make that, that
          noise --

                    MAX
          -- But it's the effort that counts,
          isn't it, Miriam? And they do enjoy
          themselves.

                    MICHAEL
          There's a lot of joy in music, Mr.
          Yasgar. And we'd love to bring the
          joy to your beautiful farm,
          wouldn't we?

Nods from the rest of the team.

                    MICHAEL (CONT'D)
          I know it's going to be something
          of an imposition, but we're more
          than willing --

                    MAX
          Yes. You say you want to use these
          fields here? Then you'll need the
          land beside the barns too, I'm
          guessing, for access to the road.

                    TISHA
          And parking.

                    MAX
          Probably best across 17B. I own the
          piece down the road, but there are
          a couple of lots, you'll probably
          want to avoid dealing with the
          Browns. And you'll clean up after
          yourselves, I suppose.

> MICHAEL
> Of course.

> MAX
> Well...

A long pause.

> MAX (CONT'D)
> Would...five thousand dollars do it
> for you?

A long pause.

> MICHAEL
> Five...

An even longer pause.

> MAX
> But you'll have to tidy up. And
> you'll have to pay for any damaged
> crops, of course.

> MICHAEL
> Sure, Max. That'd be fine.

They shake hands.

> MAX
> Wonderful. Then come on in to the
> house for some chocolate milk!

39   OMITTED   39

40   EXT. YASGUR'S FARMHOUSE -- PORCH -- DAY   40

Elliot hovers by Michael as he and the others are getting
into the limos. Michael turns back to Elliot.

> MICHAEL
> You know, we're going to need a
> place for people to crash, while we
> prepare the festival. Your place
> looks pretty cool. How many vacant
> rooms do you have for the next
> couple of weeks?

                    ELLIOT
          Well, it depends on how you define
          room.

                    MICHAEL
          You know, how many people can crash
          with you. What do you guys charge?

                    ELLIOT
          Um, let's see -- it's 8 dollars a
          night, but that can be for doubles,
          and we give a weekly discount, of
          course. Plus the cabins, you can
          get cots, so four people -- you
          could get about 150, 200 people --

Elliot tries to -- or at least pretends to -- do some
calculations in his head.

                    MICHAEL
          Hey, man, let's make it easy, why
          don't we just buy the El Monaco out
          for the season? And if we don't use
          all the rooms, you can rent out the
          free ones. We'll need to keep some
          clean up crews around afterwards.
          And if you've got some bigger
          spaces, for offices, that kind of
          thing, we'll need to put in some
          phones, have some space to park
          vehicles. Here --

Tisha hands Michael a pad of paper and pencil, which he hands
to Elliot.

                    MICHAEL (CONT'D)
          Just figure out the cost, write it
          down, and we'll take a look.

Elliot does just that, but his hand is shaking, he keeps
crossing numbers out, rewriting, making a mess of it, clearly
not doing any real math. Finally, he hands the paper to
Michael, who then shows it to Mel and a couple of the others.
They nod.

                    MICHAEL (CONT'D)
          Looks like we can work with this,
          Elli.

                    ELLIOT
               (practically falsetto)
          Cool!
                    (MORE)

                    ELLIOT (CONT'D)
          Oh, and, I was thinking, you know
          I've got that theater troupe in the
          barn.

                    STAN
          A theater troupe? In the barn?

                    ELLIOT
          Yeah, um, the Earthlight Players.
          It's ok if they stay right? Maybe
          you guys might have some work for
          them? They could really use the
          pay.

                    MICHAEL
          They're all hired, man. Not a
          problem.

He nods to Tisha, who goes into the limo and comes out with a
brown paper bag. Michael extends it to Elliot.

                    MICHAEL (CONT'D)
          And I hope you don't mind -- we
          like to pay cash, in advance.

Elliot just stares at the bag.

41   INT. EL MONACO MOTEL -- BACK ROOM -- DAY   41

Elliot is mid-stream recounting his business dealings to his
mother and father.

                    ELLIOT
          And not only that! He made me a
          local community liaison for the
          festival, AND we're going to be the
          exclusive local ticket agency too!
          They think at least 5,000 people
          will buy tickets - or more!

                    SONIA
          Five thousand coming here, to White
          Lake? Elli, you're an idiot!
          Twenty, thirty of them, ok, for a
          weekend. But a thousand, five
          thousand. They'll steal everything!
          We'll be sued in court by the
          neighbors.

                    ELLIOT
          Ma...

                         SONIA
          What kind of meshugge hairy
          barefoot person comes here in a
          heliocoptic that we should lay our
          good white sheets on the grass and
          ruin them, and then plot and
          revolutionize to take our hotel --

                         ELLIOT
          Ma, he pays cash --

                         SONIA
          Everyone pays cash here, you
          schnook!

                         ELLIOT
          No, ma, really...

Elliot places the paper bag on the table.

                         ELLIOT (CONT'D)
          Open it.

She gingerly peeks into the bag.

                         ELLIOT (CONT'D)
          Open it. That's $5,000 for the
          rent, and another $25,000 for my
          services as liaison! Plus think of
          what we might make on commissions
          for the ticket sales!

Sonia, as if in a trance, lays out the money, bundled in neat
stacks, onto the table in front of them.

                         ELLIOT (CONT'D)
          And also --

                         SONIA
          Schush!

She starts to count it.

The phone rings.

Elliot gets it.

                         ELLIOT
          El Monaco International Casino and
          Bar Mitzvah Center....Max! Hi Max!
          What's that?

41A   INTERCUT YASGUR'S FARMHOUSE KITCHEN - DAY: 41A

                         MAX
               Elliot. Look, the phone hasn't
               stopped ringing since you left. You
               know, they're saying thousands of
               people might come!

                         ELLIOT
               Yeah, Max, that's...wow.

                         MAX
               Well, Elliot, it's going to cost
               quite a bit just to get everything
               back in order. And to get the cows
               situated.

                         ELLIOT
               I can understand, sure.

                         MAX
               Trust me, Elliot, I don't wish to
               mess up your festival, you know
               that. And I think what was done to
               those young people in Wallkill was
               just plain wrong. But I've spoken
               with Miriam, and we think, if you
               could tell those people...

                         ELLIOT
               How much?

                         MAX
               Seventy-five thousand. Not a penny
               less.

                         ELLIOT
                    (feeling faint)
               Ok, Max. I'll let them know.

He hangs up the phone slowly, turns to his parents.

                         SONIA
               What?

                         ELLIOT
               Ma, don't spend any of that yet.
               That was Max, the deal's off.

                         SONIA
               What?! Impossible!

She instantly scoops up the money and hightails it into the other room.

> ELLIOT
> Mom!

> JAKE
> Don't try to stop her, Elliot. She
> can't get far.

42   INT./EXT. YASGUR'S FARMHOUSE -- KITCHEN -- DAY   42

Close on Michael Lang:

> MICHAEL
> Hey, that's cool.

Wider: Elliot, Michael Lang, and some of the other Woodstock team are gathered at the counter facing Max and Miriam. JOEL ROSENMAN (smart, open face) and JOHN ROBERTS (somewhat more conservative, trust-fund kid, friendly, still in the army reserves so his hair is noticeably shorter than everyone else's) have also joined -- it's John's trust fund money that's paying for Woodstock, and Joel is his friend and business partner.

> MAX
> And I read in the paper this
> morning, you already sold thousands
> of tickets. That's a lot, and
> you'll be needing to use
> practically my whole place here,
> not just the alfalfa fields.

A long silence.

> JOHN
> Now, wait a second. I mean, I could
> fu-- I mean, I could <u>buy</u> a farm for
> the kind of money you're asking. I
> could buy <u>five</u> farms.

Max just smiles at him.

> MAX
> From what the papers say, Mr.
> Roberts, you've already spent a
> million dollars down in Wallkill,
> and you've only got until the 15th
> until your festival.
> (MORE)

                    MAX (CONT'D)
Now I'm sure a wealthy young man
such as yourself could indeed buy a
lot of farms. I'm just saying --

          JOEL
-- Yeah, you're just saying you've
got us over a barrel.

          MAX
If I didn't, you wouldn't be on
your second carton of chocolate
milk there, would ya? But I tell
you this, when you make a deal with
me, it's a deal. So long as you
promise to put everything back in
order, I'll stand by you a hundred
percent. I won't let anyone run you
off like they did in Wallkill,
either. This is my land and let's
just see 'em try.

          MICHAEL
Wow Max, that is very cool. And
you're right, we're going to have a
lot of people come and enjoy your
place.

          JOHN
Michael, if I may, I wouldn't
describe $75,000 as cool.

          JOEL
$5,000 is cool.

          MICHAEL
Hey, it's your bread, guys. I'm
just trying to put you together
here with Max's vision.

John and Joel roll their eyes, turn back to Max. As they
continue to haggle with him, Elliot tries to get Michael's
attention, waving him and Tisha over to the front door.

          ELLIOT
Uh, Mike..Mike.

          JOEL
Right. Look, Max. If we were
willing to consider this, you're
gonna have to really let us make it
work -- we're gonna have to bring
electricity, water --

                    MAX
You mean dig trenches? No, no
trenches.

                    JOEL
What? You're kidding.

                    MAX
Pipes will have to stay above
ground. And of course you won't
build anything permanent.

                    ELLIOT
          (whispering, to Mike)
Mike, really, if this doesn't shake
out with Max, I'm sure we can find
you another spot, no problem.

                    MICHAEL
Hey, Elliot, I really appreciate
your optimism, but it's all going
to be fine. John and Joel and Max,
they're all gonna come together, I
can feel it. Good vibes.

Michael wanders back to the negotiation. Elliot keeps Tisha
back with him.

                    ELLIOT
Can I ask you a question?

                    TISHA
Please.

                    ELLIOT
Is Mike for real? I mean, he's just
so...relaxed.

                    TISHA
Michael, yeah, he's totally real --
so long as the cash is real -- and
the cash is real so long as John
and Joel are real. And I guess
John and Joel are gonna stay real
'cause between us, they already
sold 100,000 tickets, and who wants
100,000 freaks coming after them
for refunds?

                    ELLIOT
100,000! Wow.

They hear yelling from the other side of the room. (Most of the following dialogue will not be heard, but just run in the background.)

                    MAX
          You can pump the water out of the
          lake. That's good fresh water.

                    JOHN
          Not after 50,000 people take a bath
          in it.

                    MAX
          They'll certainly not be allowed in
          the lake. And in any case, Smithson
          won't let them near it.

                    JOEL
          Smithson?

                    MAX
          That's not my property down there?

                    JOEL
          No?

                    MAX
          This is, and that. And about the
          alfalfa --

                    JOHN
          What about the alfalfa.

                    MAX
          Can't touch it. Which reminds me,
          I'm sure you'll be willing to put
          up a bond, just in case there's
          damage -- I was thinking $75,000.

                    JOEL
          Fuck! A $75,0000 bond too?

He gives Michael a dirty look.

                    TISHA
          Wow, that Max Yasgur -- now _he's_
          real.

44 INT. SLATTERY'S DRUG STORE -- DAY 44

Elliot enters, goes to sit at the counter.

The place goes silent.

He looks up to see everyone, including Dan, and a few other
familiar faces, staring at him.

> ELLIOT
> Hello?

No one says a word.

Dave comes up.

> ELLIOT (CONT'D)
> Hey Dave. I'll have the usual.

> DAVE
> Sorry Elliot. I think we're out of
> the usual.

> ELLIOT
> Out of the usual? (trying to kid)
> Wow, that's unusual.

From down the counter, Dan pipes up.

> DAN
> For crying out loud, Elliot! How
> could you?

> ELLIOT
> Ok, I'll try the waffles.

> DAN
> Don't get cute.

Dan gets up and thrusts a newspaper in his hand. Elliot looks
at it -- a full page ad, with a caricature cartoon of a
couple of hicks, Elliot softly reads aloud the text:

> ELLIOT
> "To insure three days of peace and
> music, we've left Wallkill and are
> now in White Lake, New
> York....Certain people of Wallkill
> decided to try to run us out of
> town...Our new site, it's twice the
> size of our original site...uh..."

                    BOB
          You did this, Teichberg!

                    DAN
          You know what those hippies are
          going to do to this town?

                    BOB
          They'll be high on drugs. Robbing
          us by day and raping the cattle at
          night!

Other voices join into the chorus of disapproval.

                    OTHERS
          We oughtta run you Jews outta town!
          You and Yasgur! We're gonna boycott
          Yasgur's milk!

Elliot quickly gets up and runs out of the store.

45   EXT. SLATTERY'S DRUG STORE -- DAY   45

As Elliot exits, he runs right into Annie and Marge.

                    ANNIE
          Elliot!

                    ELLIOT
          Hi Annie!

                    ANNIE
          God bless you! You can't imagine
          what's happened this morning!

                    ELLIOT
          What?

                    ANNIE
          I'm fully booked! Every room!

                    MARGARET
          Me too! For the first time since
          Herb died! Thank you, Elliot!

                    ELLIOT
          You're welcome!

Annie and Margaret enter the store. Elliot takes a deep
breath and looks up to see Billy leaning against his car.

                    BILLY
          Those motherfuckers in there wanna
          fuck you up, huh?

                    ELLIOT
          Yeah, that seems to be the sense
          I'm getting.

                    BILLY
          You're gonna have to carve some
          fuckin' hearts out, man, and fry
          'em on a stick over a fire pit --
          and then sit down and eat 'em,
          before those motherfuckers do the
          aforesaid fucking to you, man!

                    ELLIOT
          Billy, can you stop with the
          motherfucking this and
          motherfucking that. Please?

That's enough to give Billy pause. He becomes calmer.

                    BILLY
          Fuck.

                    ELLIOT
          Yeah. Fuck.

                    BILLY
          This could really be a down trip.
          My brother and his wife, they're
          getting fucking organized.

                    ELLIOT
          Your brother?

                    BILLY
          Sucks, huh? You're fucking with his
          fishing, man -- he doesn't like
          that.

                    ELLIOT
          Then what should I do?

                    BILLY
          Get fuckin organized yourself.
          Rally your troops.

                    ELLIOT
          Do I have troops?

                         BILLY
          Sure. You got your mom, she's a
          fuckin battalion.

                         ELLIOT
          Huh. And the chamber of commerce.
          This whole thing is commerce,
          right?

                         BILLY
          Right on!

                         ELLIOT
          That's right...on.

Elliot distractedly gets into his car.

                         ELLIOT (CONT'D)
          It's off to HQ. (notices Billy) At
          ease, men...man.

                         BILLY
          Go fry those fuckers. Elliot!

Billy watches him drive off.

                         BILLY (CONT'D)
                    (under his breath)
          Fuck.

45A   INT. WOODSTOCK VENTURES OFFICE -- DAY   45A

       The walls are demolished.

46   EXT. EL MONACO MOTEL -- DAY   46

       Elliot drives into the parking lot. He parks next to a phone
       company truck and a couple of other cars, sees phone company
       workers rolling out cable.

       NOTE: From now on, each time we return to the El Monaco we'll
       notice a decided increase in traffic and activity.

47   OMITTED   47

48   OMITTED   48

49   OMITTED   49

50   OMITTED   50

51   INT. EL MONACO MOTEL -- FRONT OFFICE -- DAY   51

Jake and Sonia stare across the counter, facing a young
hippie couple.

                    HIPPIE GUY
          Hey.

Long pause.

                    JAKE
          Hey.

                    HIPPIE GIRL
          We were in Wallkill.

                    HIPPIE GUY
          Hanging with some friends, making
          the scene.

                    HIPPIE GIRL
          Rapping on each other.

                    HIPPIE GUY
          And they said this is where it's
          at.

                    HIPPIE GIRL
          So we rode our thumbs up here.

                    HIPPIE GUY
          Can you dig it?

Elliot enters.

                    JAKE
          Elliot, help!

                    SONIA
          It's these two -- They want a hole -
          -

                    JAKE
          -- to dig their thumbs --

                    SONIA
          -- After they hit each other, they
          made a scene in Wallkill!

                    ELLIOT
               (confused, to the couple)
          What are they talking about?

                    HIPPIE GUY
          Just looking to score...you know,
          the magic tickets...

                    ELLIOT
          Ah, dad. Get the tickets! To the
          festival.

Jake finds the ticket and cash box.

Elliot rolls his eyes and exits.

52   EXT. EL MONACO MOTEL -- FRONT OFFICE -- DAY   52

          Elliot pauses in front of the door he's just closed behind
          him. He hears screams of joy from inside. He looks through
          the window and sees the hippie girl giving his father a big
          hug and kiss. His father steps back, incredulous.

52A   INT. BETHEL CHURCH BASEMENT -- NIGHT   52A

          Another meeting of the Chamber of Commerce. Elliot sits at
          the table facing Marge and Annie and a couple of other locals
          in the empty hall. There's an eerie silence.

                    ANNIE
               (clearing her throat)
          I have a motion.

                    ELLIOT
          Great. Before you make your motion,
          let me call the meeting to order.

Just then, the back doors open and scores of locals, led by a
clearly angry Dan and Carol, silently march into the hall and
take their sits or stand along the hallways. Elliot,
extremely nervous, continues on.

                    ELLIOT (CONT'D)
          So, the meeting is now called to
          order. Um, approval of the minutes.

                    ANNIE
          Even better than the last ones.

                    ELLIOT
          Thank you Annie.

                  ELLIOT (CONT'D)
          Old business.....

Silence.

                  ELLIOT (CONT'D)
          None. Excellent.

Elliot takes a deep breath.

                  ELLIOT (CONT'D)
          Um....New business?

The room erupts in shouting from every corner, above which we
hear Dan.

                  DAN
          You better fucking believe there's
          new business, Elliot! Let's start
          with how you and Yasgar invited a
          mob of dope-smoking zombies to come
          and destroy our town! Don't think
          you're going to get away with this!

                  TOWNSPEOPLE
           (ad libs)
          You and your whore mother will be
          back in Siberia before those
          hippies ever get here! Who paid you
          off, Tiber? This used to be a nice
          community, and now! You and your
          permits -- you don't have the right
          to issue permits! What Chamber of
          Commerce anywhere issues permits?!

                  ELLIOT
          Guys! Guys! Just...Please...

More shouts and abuse are hurled at Elliot.

Suddenly, Elliot stands up.

                  ELLIOT (CONT'D)
           (a loud shout)
          Hold on a minute!

The room falls silent. No one's ever seen Elliot so forceful -
- indeed, he can't really believe he shut them up himself.

                  ELLIOT (CONT'D)
          (realizing he's now got to
         give a speech)
          (MORE)

ELLIOT (CONT'D)
Just...I mean...What's wrong with
you people? Look around. Our town
is on the brink of annihilation.
There's no tourist industry here,
no traffic, no business, no one to
pay taxes for our schools and
facilities. And now a golden goose
has mysteriously landed at Max
Yasgar's farm, with enough golden
eggs to feed us all. White Lake is
going to be back on the map, with
ten thousand people or more with
cash in their pockets, all coming
to spend it here!

He pauses, looking around the room. For a moment, we think
he's swayed them, a la Jimmy Stewart in a Frank Capra movie.
A couple of nodding heads, but then...

TOWNSPEOPLE
What a load of crap! Up yours, you
scheming bastard! You think we'd
take money from that trash?! Ok,
maybe he's got a point, but who
pays for the clean up? It's not
like the town gets any sales tax.
Normal people won't make any money.
We'll take this to the supreme
court!

Dan gets everybody to quiet down a bit.

DAN
Hold it! Ok! Ok! So what are we
going to do about it?

Everyone turns to Elliot.

ELLIOT
Uh, meeting adjourned!

The place erupts again. Annie leans over toward Elliot.

ANNIE
Probably best if you leave by the
back door, dear.

52AA   INT. EL MONACO MOTEL - BACK ROOM -- NIGHT   52AA

Jake and Sonia sit, somewhat zombified, in the glow of the tv
set, glued to the screen, We can't see what they're watching.

                        TV ANNOUNCER
                And there...he steps off the
                ladder...a little hop...

Jake and Sonia hear something in the doorway, look up, and
see Elliot, dejected standing there. They turn their eyes
back to the tv. Elliot's regard follows theirs.

On the tv:

Images of the first walk on the moon.

52B   EXT. EL MONACO MOTEL -- DAY   52B

Tisha comes up to Elliot.

                        ELLIOT
                Hi Tisha. What is it?

                        TISHA
                You've got a couple of visitors.

52C   EXT. EL MONACO MOTEL -- BEHIND THE MAIN BUILDING -- DAY   52C

Elliot and Tisha round the corner of the main building to
find two middle-aged, straight-laced men, standing, filling
out forms on clipboards.

                        ELLIOT
                Hello? What can I do for you?

                        INSPECTOR #1
                Mr. Teichberg?

                        ELLIOT
                Yes?

                        INSPECTOR #1
                    (handing him a stack of
                     papers)
                Here. That's forty-seven citations -
                - wiring, plumbing, health code
                violations. Quite a place you've
                got here.

                        ELLIOT
                It's humble but its home... Away
                from home...I mean.

                    INSPECTOR #2
          And here's fourteen more -- fire
          code. You're way over the occupancy
          limits.

Elliot, in shock, fumbles through the stack.

                    INSPECTOR #1
          You've got five days to pay up and
          repair -- or else we're shutting
          you down for good.

                    INSPECTOR #2
          Have a nice day.

Snickering, they amble off.

52D   EXT. EL MONACO MOTEL -- DAY   52D

Elliot strides across the lawn, clutching the health
department citations in one hand.

The place is even more abuzz with activity. There are now
trailers parked in the drive, workers and volunteers bustling
about.

He spots his father entering a room carrying a shower
curtain. He follows his father into the room, noticing that
the sign next to the door has been changed from "Room 17" to
"Rooms 17A and 17B."

52E   INT. EL MONACO MOTEL -- ROOM -- DAY   52E

Inside, he sees Jake and Sonia rigging a curtain over a
clothesline strung up in the middle of the room.

                    ELLIOT
          What's going on?

                    JAKE
          Your mother says we can double our
          money...

                    SONIA
          Two times the rooms.

                    ELLIOT
          You're kidding me.

                    JAKE
          They don't seem to mind. Honest,
          these people, they like it.

                    ELLIOT
              Uh!

He turns and goes.

53   INT. EL MONACO MOTEL -- WOODSTOCK OFFICES -- DAY   53

A makeshift command center and field office is in the process
of being thrown together. Elliot enters. He finds Michael
Lang going over some papers with Tisha and the team.

                    ELLIOT
          Mike, hi, if you have a second. I'm
          just a little anxious -- did Tisha
          tell you about these code
          violations --

                    MICHAEL
          Hey Elliot. Just the man I want to
          see. You know, I'm getting the
          feeling we're really going to be
          able to use your community
          relations skills --

                    ELLIOT
          -- My what skills? Did someone tell
          you about the meeting?

                    MICHAEL
          You had a meeting? Cool. Because,
          Elli, the rumors are already
          swirling, and we gotta put a local
          face on the reality here, and you,
          Elli, are a local face --

                    ELLIOT
          -- I'm a local face, yes, but about
          these violations -- I mean, there's
          not a hotel around for miles that
          could pass inspection.

                    MICHAEL
          Those inspector dudes? -- Don't
          worry about that, Elli. Tisha told
          me all about those guys. Just give
          us the papers. We've got some heavy
          lawyers. And --

He nods to Tisha. She holds up another paper bag...

Michael smiles.

>   MICHAEL (CONT'D)
>   Yeah, heavy lawyers -- because
>   right now I need you to focus all
>   your energy on the positive message
>   we're sending, you know, rapping
>   with the townspeople, making time
>   with some of the local papers here -
>   -

>   ELLIOT
>   Wait, you mean, like, a press
>   conference?

>   MICHAEL
>   A press conference -- hey, radical
>   idea, Elli. I love it.

>   ELLIOT
>   No, actually, you don't. Me and
>   public speaking, I can guarantee
>   you, just not really one of my
>   strong suits. I'm speaking from
>   experience here.

>   MICHAEL
>   Hey, I want you to meet someone.

Michael puts his arm around Elliot and they walk to the other side of the room, past various people at work. We overhear their conversations and meetings in the background:

>   JOHN MORRIS
>   Don't ask me why it's called
>   Woodstock. Everyone's gonna drive
>   to the fuckin' real Woodstock and
>   be really bummed when they get
>   there --

>   PENNY
>   D-o-t's letting us put up signage,
>   just not on the thruway yet, but
>   we're working it.

A few chairs down, Stan talks to Wes Pomeroy, a distinguished looking man who heads security, and Mel Lawrence:

>   STAN
>   Wavy Gravy and the Hog Farmers --

                    WES
Wavy?

                    STAN
Wavy Gravy -- real name's Hugh.
He's got 80 freaks -- the Hog
Farmers --

                    WES
They fog harms? I mean --

                    STAN
-- No, they hog farms, I mean farm
hogs -- but no, I mean they don't,
they just call themselves that.
They've got a commune in the
desert, see? -- and they drop more
acid than Timothy Leary. There's 80
of 'em coming in on a jumbo jet
next week to come in and set up
camps, free kitchens, trip tents --

                    WES
Trip tents...

                    STAN
Where the kids can come down --

                    WES
From their trips.

                    STAN
And Wavy --

                    WES
-- Gravy --

                    STAN
He and his people are willing to
work with you on security - they
really like your non-
confrontational approach -- you
know, they wanna call it a "please
force".

                    WES
Not so sure Fabbri's going to like
that moniker - we're still going to
need real police.

And in another corner, Chip Monck and Steve Cohen are
talking:

CHIP
(pointing at a sketch)
Can you trench here? --

STEVE COHEN
No, everything, water pipes, juice,
gotta run all the cable above
ground --

Back to Penny, on the phone:

PENNY
Joyce, he doesn't even know what a
purchase order is....How much?
(writing) All right. Did John put
more funds in that account or
should I use the other one?

CHIP
-- I got the specs from Hanley, for
the speakers --

STEVE COHEN
(looking at the specs)
Lotta juice --

CHIP
When Hendrix lights up, there won't
be a bird left in Sullivan County.

Michael continues to pitch Elliot:

MICHAEL
Let me introduce you to Reverend
Don. He's helping with our
community outreach and he'd love it
if you could help him get to know
the locals...

Don, an ex-priest with a casual air, rises.

>   DON
>   Hey. So glad to meet you. I don't
>   know how much Mike's told you, but
>   we're thinking of putting on a
>   little free performance for the
>   local people here, and we thought
>   it would be a great idea to include
>   a scene from your theater company.
>   Do you think they'd be open to it?

>   ELLIOT
>   (getting overwhelmed)
>   Yeah, they'd love that. But, you
>   said for the locals? Because the
>   play's very...contemporary --

But before Elliot can finish Don is waylaid by an assistant
with a note pad, and then:

The sound of ringing phones.

>   ASSISTANT
>   (shouting)
>   The phones are alive!

Cheers all around as everyone dives into work.

Elliot just takes it in for a second, when another assistant
calls out.

>   ASSISTANT 2
>   Is Elliot here? Your dad wants you!

54   EXT. EL MONACO MOTEL -- BUNGALOW -- DAY   54

Elliot and Jake march across the bustling grounds. In the
background, we see a bunch of volunteers and workers
stripping down to their underwear and jumping into the pool.

They reach a cottage, which has been covered with graffiti --
swastikas, "Tichberg -- Your Days Are Numbered" "Commies Go
Home" "Faggot Jews"

Jake points down the hill and across the road to a small
group of young local red-necks hanging about, clearly happy
to make themselves known as the culprits.

>   ELLIOT
>   I'll get some paint -- but they're
>   just going to do it again.

                    JAKE
          They set foot here again, I break
          their heads.

                    ELLIOT
          Dad, let me call --

                    JAKE
          Call who? That little putz in the
          green shirt, that's the son of that
          state trooper! I could boil him and
          his putz of a father in tar.

                    ELLIOT
          Just, dad, let's get this painted
          before mom sees it. Then you can
          start warming up the tar.

55   INT. EL MONACO MOTEL -- BACK ROOM -- DAY   55

Sonia is sitting in front of the tv, watching the news.
Vietnam again, Nixon, etc. But her ears perk up when she sees
coverage of the Sharon Tate murders in L.A. -- a band of
murderous hippies is on the loose.

                    TV REPORTER #2
          We have unconfirmed reports that
          William Garretson, the caretaker at
          the Sharon Tate house, has been
          taken into custody for the grisly
          murders there, as film director
          Roman Polanski arrived today from
          London for his pregnant wife's
          funeral. Police, however, warn,
          that these savage murders were most
          likely not the work of a single
          killer but of a group of ritual
          subversives, driven by their hatred
          of the establishment, the police,
          and all authority.

She gets up, looks out her window, sees four or five hippies
sitting on the grass, passing a water pipe. She quickly pulls
down the shades. She looks over to see Jake rummaging around
in the closet -- he pulls out a baseball bat, weighs it in
his hands.

56   INT. EL MONACO MOTEL -- BAR AREA -- NIGHT   56

Jake serves drinks to a group of festival workers at the bar,
furiously collecting cash. Elliot is stacking bottles and
bags of snacks.

                    JAKE
          Put some more of those in the
          cooler.

                    ELLIOT
          Dad. This is all we got.

                    JAKE
          You didn't order more?

                    ELLIOT
          I did. And I called Karpen's too,
          for the kitchen. I asked them all
          to bring ten times our usual.

                    JAKE
               (thinking)
          When they come tomorrow, tell them
          to bring twenty times more...no,
          thirty times.

                    ELLIOT
          Where are we going to put it all?

                    JAKE
          These people eat and drink like
          animals, and there's more of them
          every minute. It'll be gone in a
          day.

Across the room, one of the Woodstock guys is setting up a
record player and some speakers. Elliot goes over, as the
speakers come to life with a small blast.

                    ELLIOT
          You got that thing working?

                    PAUL
               (hunky, sweet)
          Yeah. Just don't touch those wires.
               (noticing a stack of
                records)
          What you got to put on?

                    ELLIOT
               (a bit awkward)
          Nothing much.

                    PAUL
          Hey. Judy Garland. Carnegie Hall.
          Haven't heard that in a long time.

                    ELLIOT
               (sensing a possible
                kindred soul)
          Hard to believe she's gone.
          Actually, I can believe it. I met
          her once.

                    PAUL
          Wow. Was she fat?

                    ELLIOT
          She was...brimming...over... I'm
          Elliot.

                    PAUL
          Paul. Construction. You seen the
          stage we're building? Huge.

                    ELLIOT
          Wow. Want another beer?

                    PAUL
          No thanks. I've got a thing going
          with some Lebanese Red right now.
          Your old man doesn't mind if we
          light up in here?

                    ELLIOT
          He can't smell anything -- too much
          roofing tar.

                    PAUL
          Cool.

Elliot watches him walk back to the group, then glances at
his father, watching him, a neutral expression on his face.

57   OMITTED   57

58   EXT. EL MONACO MOTEL -- SWAMPY LAWN -- DAY   58

Sonia is directing a van full of hippies as it backs into a
spot near the lake. She keeps motioning for it to pull back
further, next to another parked car with a tent set up beside
it.

                    SONIA
          More...more.

As the van backs in, it begins to sink deeply into the swampy
muck.

                    SONIA (CONT'D)
          Uh...ok. Good! Forty dollars.

The driver hands over a wad of crumpled bills. Sonia looks up
to see Elliot coming down the hill -- behind him, we see
activity, people, trucks everywhere.

                    ELLIOT
          Ma! Tisha says you're trying to
          charge extra for pillows and soap
          again. We talked about this!

58A   EXT. WOODY PATH - DAY   58A
They begin to walk back to the motel together.

                    SONIA
          Don't accuse me! I have nothing to
          sell anyway, not even toilet paper!

                    ELLIOT
          Which leads me to ask -- where do
          you think all these people you're
          renting space to are going to do
          their business? You've got to stop,
          mom -- enough with the money. We
          just paid the mortgage off, think
          about it! Be happy!

But Sonia is not paying attention. She's noticed a rustling
behind some bushes, and picks up a stick and starts poking.
We hear a cry of pain and see the shapes of two semi-naked
young people rise and run off.

                    SONIA
          Hey! No shtupping in the bushes!

Elliot, frustrated, strides toward the main office building,
his mother huffing behind them.

58B   EXT. EL MONACO MOTEL -- DAY   58B
        A line of hippies in front of the office, ten or 15 strong.

                    HIPPIE IN LINE
              (as Elliot and Sonia pass)
            Excuse me, when does the ticket
            office open?

                    SONIA
            Not yet! Soon!

        At the pay phone, a young man beseeches into the receiver:

                    YOUNG GUY AT PHONE
            Mom, you gotta talk to dad....No,
            no one stole the car, I just gotta
            keep it for a few days. Sure it's
            legal!

59   INT. EL MONACO MOTEL -- FRONT OFFICE -- DAY   59

        Elliot enters, his mother behind him, to find a couple of
        tough guys squared off against Jake.

                    CHARLIE
            Good morning. You must be the
            lovely wife and child.

        Jake looks scared.

                    ELLIOT
            What's up, dad?

                    CHARLIE
            We were just telling your pops here
            -- looks like you guys are getting
            some nice business.

                    ELLIOT
            Yeah?

                    CHARLIE
            So it looks like you could use some
            help.

                    ELLIOT
            We already hired a bunch of kids to
            help out -- we're all hired up.

                    JAKE
          He's talking nonsense, Elli.
          Something about exclusive
          transportation and security -- for
          $10,000!!

                    ELLIOT
          Oh. I get it.

                    DOUG
          No, you don't get it -- WE get it.
          You got live entertainment
          happening here, beverages,
          etcetera.

                    CHARLIE
          We cover the hotels around the
          racetrack in Monticello, we cover
          you.

                    JAKE
          And what if I say you don't?

                    DOUG
          Uh, Charlie, what if he says we
          don't?

                    JAKE
          You're trespassers. Get out, or I
          make you get out!

                    DOUG
             (menacing)
          Is that so?

                    JAKE
             (to Sonia)
          You hear this? Enough with these
          bums!

With that, Jake grabs the baseball bat from behind the
counter, and takes a wild swing at Charlie, missing by a
mile. Charlie lets out a malicious chuckle as Doug approaches
Jake.

                    ELLIOT
          Dad, you can barely walk, what are
          you doing?

But as Doug gets closer, Sonia charges both him and Charlie
from the side, knocking the one into the other. Off balance,
they're not prepared for Jake's second swing, which catches
one of them behind the knees.

He goes down as Sonia pushes the other one over him. Jake then takes a swing at Doug, who, now scared, starts backing out of the room.

                    DOUG
          Whoa! Ok, ok!

But now Elliot sees Charlie charge at Sonia --

                    ELLIOT
          Ma, watch out!

Elliot jumps on Charlie's back as Sonia kicks him between the legs, again and again. Elliot tumbles off him and flies into the corner.

                    CHARLIE
          Jesus, all right! You people are
          animals!

Doug helps Charlie up to his feet, and they back out the door.

60   EXT. EL MONACO MOTEL -- DAY   60

As the goons exit, past the queue of confused hippies waiting for tickets, Jake, Sonia and Elliot walk out after them, Jake still brandishing the bat.

                    JAKE
          Get out! And if you ever try to
          come back, we won't be so nice the
          next time!

They run/walk to the road.

Elliot looks, amazed at his parents.

                    ELLIOT
          Dad, mom -- you're...superheroes!

                    JAKE
          My arthritis is killing me.

                    SONIA
          I told you not to stand at the bar
          all night.

                    JAKE
          You didn't tell me anything.

                         SONIA
               You're deaf. How would you know
               what I tell you?

They walk back into the motel as Elliot stands there,
dumbfounded.

Behind him, in line, we discover a statuesque, somewhat gone-
to-seed middle-aged blonde in an incongruous summer dress,
watching the whole show. This is VILMA, whom we shall get to
know shortly. Elliot notices her briefly before hearing his
name called by Michael.

61   INT. EL MONACO MOTEL -- WOODSTOCK OFFICES -- DAY   61

                         MICHAEL
               Just thought we should go over a
               couple of things before the
               conference.

                         ELLIOT
               The...conference?

                         MICHAEL
               Your press conference, man.

                         ELLIOT
               Oh, right.

                         MICHAEL
               Relax. You're gonna be great. Just
               be yourself. People are gonna
               respond to your reality, your local
               reality, and that's important.
               Because we're giving birth here to
               a whole new nation, the Woodstock
               nation!

                         ELLIOT
               Ok!

                         DON
               Now they're going to ask you about
               ticket sales and numbers.

                         ELLIOT
               Yeah, that's right. My dad says
               we're already running out of the
               tickets you gave us.

                    MICHAEL
          Cool. That's great. More coming.
          The thing is, word is getting out
          that maybe we'll have a few more
          guests than we originally thought --

                    STAN
          Yeah, like a hundred thousand more -
          -

                    ELLIOT
          What?

                    MICHAEL
          It's great. All the major artists
          have signed up --

                    ARTIE
          Like everybody --

                    MICHAEL
          And we're ordering more toilets.

                    ARTIE
          For sure. Toilets, yeah.

                    ELLIOT
          Oh. Can we have some?

                    MICHAEL
          So there may be some public opinion
          pressure --

                    DON
          That's why on Friday, you can
          announce, we're holding a free
          event for the community. Some
          school bands, and a couple of
          excellent professional acts --

                    ARTIE
          Except not Train, no..

                    ELLIOT
          Train?

                    ARTIE
          Not Train...No, Train are angry.

                    MICHAEL
          Yeah, Train are very angry.

                    ARTIE
          Quill. Quill is far out.

                    ELLIOT
          So there will be a lot of toilets,
          you want me to say? But no Train?

                    ARTIE
          No. Quill. And a lot of public
          initiatives...A petting zoo for
          kids.

John and Robert enter the office as they are talking, and
come over.

                    JOEL
          We need to get over to Yasgar's --

                    STAN
          -- I'll take you.

                    JOHN
          Thanks. Mel says there's already a
          couple of thousand people camping
          out on the site.

                    MICHAEL
          Yeah. Everyone's eating Max's
          delicious yoghurt.

                    JOEL
          That's nice, Michael. But while we
          spend $25,000 putting up a fence
          around them -- and the thousands
          more who are joining them every day
          -- has anyone asked any of these
          people if perhaps they're planning
          on buying tickets?

                    ARTIE
          That is a good question, man.

                    JOHN
               (kindly satiric, to Joel)
          That is a good question, Joel.

                    JOEL
          Thanks, John.

                    JOHN
          Thank you, Joel.

Everyone is up and going, except Elliot, who sits befuddled.
Tisha comes and sits next to him.

> ELLIOT
> Hi Tisha...

> TISHA
> Hey Elliot.

> ELLIOT
> I was noticing that John and Joel
> seem particularly real today.

> TISHA
> (sardonic)
> Yeah, they're achieving a whole new
> level of reality. C'mon. Michael
> needs you to make an introduction.

62   INT. BETHEL BANK - DAY   62

A small line of local farmers and merchants await the sole
teller.

The front door opens and Elliot, accompanied by a barefoot
Michael, carrying a leather travel bag, enter.

Immediately, the place gets an ugly feel to it.

Jackson spots Elliot and Michael, and rushes over to them.

> JACKSON
> (loud whisper, freaked)
> Elliot! What are you doing here?

> ELLIOT
> I wanted to introduce you to Mike
> Lang, from Woodstock Ventures.

> JACKSON
> The concert? Are you crazy?
> (taking them into a
> corner.)
> I can't be seen with you people --
> I'll be lynched.

> ELLIOT
> Mr. Lang wishes to open an account,
> a business account. He'll need
> payroll services, secure cash
> transport, and he needs everything
> set up by this afternoon.

                    JACKSON
          Elliot, look outside, it's a Sharon
          Tate suspects convention, we're all
          going to be killed in our sleep --

                    MICHAEL
          -- And I can open the account
          immediately with this cash deposit -
          - will $250,000 do to get us
          started?

He subtly shows him the contents of the bag. Jackson almost
keels over. He turns back to the room.

                    JACKSON
               (yelling)
          Everyone! Listen up! The bank is
          closed for, for deposit box
          maintenance! We'll be open again in
          one hour! Mary, close your cash
          box! Everyone, out! Sorry!

A number of muttered epithets from the customers as they're
pushed out the door. After the last one exits, Jackson turns
with a smile.

                    JACKSON (CONT'D)
          Mr. Lang, right this way!

63   EXT. YASGUR'S FARM -- DAY   63

Elliot pulls up and gets out of his car. The place is in the
process of its transformation. Tractors plowing, new road
being gravelled, port-a-potties being installed. Elliot walks
into a grove overlooking the campsite. He's joined by Max,
who takes out his pipe and lights it. They look over the tent
city being constructed below them.

                    MAX
          Well, Elliot? What do you think of
          the mess we're making? Wonderful,
          isn't it?

                    ELLIOT
          It is, Max. I'm just sorry everyone
          in town hates our guts now -- yours
          more than mine, if that's possible.

                    MAX
          Sorry? Hell, these kids are
          fantastic.
               (MORE)

                    MAX (CONT'D)
          I've heard more thank yous and
          pleases the past three days than
          I've heard in a lifetime from those
          schmucks. And believe me, no matter
          what they say they're all trying to
          make money on this thing too. I saw
          Bob charge a dollar to fill a
          bottle with water for one of these
          kids.

                    ELLIOT
          A dollar?

                    MAX
          Yep. Can you believe it? A dollar --
          for water!

Another look over the campsite and the happy young people
hanging out below.

On the field beside the campsite, they see Michael Lang on a
tractor, trailed by a 16mm camera crew, filming him. He
waves.

63A   EXT. BETHEL TOWN MONTAGE -- DAY   63A

We follow Elliot as he wanders the town, watching the young
people as they drive and hike in; seeing the locals setting
up makeshift stalls selling food and water; the 16mm film
crew filming some of the Hog Farmers setting up their
kitchens, etc.

64   EXT. EL MONACO MOTEL -- DAY   64

Elliot pulls up, but has to park on the lawn as there's now
no room in the parking lot.

As he heads back to his cabin, Vilma walks along side him.

                    VILMA
               (husky)
          You're Elliot, Elliot Tiber?

                    ELLIOT
          That's me.
               (still walking)
          How can I help you, Miss...?

                    VILMA
          Baroness...Von Vilma.

                    ELLIOT
          Von Vilma?

                    VILMA
          You can call me Vilma. You like the
          name?

Elliot slows down as they get near his cabin. He regards
Vilma -- it dawns on him, she's a bit different.

                    ELLIOT
          It's unique.

                    VILMA
          Exactly.

                    ELLIOT
          So what brings you here?

                    VILMA
          I'm supposed to say hi from Steve.

                    ELLIOT
          Steve?

                    VILMA
          From the village! He's gone now --
          off to San Francisco, with a flower
          in his hair. Or a sugar daddy on
          his lap. Actually, my ex sugar
          daddy, good riddance. Steve does
          like them mean and rich, doesn't
          he? Anyhow, he said you might be
          starting some sort of gay resort
          out here, and resorting, as well as
          reclining, is my specialty. And as
          I was on my way to visit my mother
          in Buffalo I thought I'd stop by --
          and look what I stumbled into! By
          the way, those clowns you and your
          dear parents chased off this
          morning? Not nice people. I know. I
          was playing the horses, if you know
          what I mean, over by the racetrack
          in Monticello. Nice little bedroom
          community -- until that bunch
          wanted to confiscate my earnings.

                    ELLIOT
          You think they'll be back?

                    VILMA
          All I can say is, you need help.

                    ELLIOT
          What kind of help?

Vilma, bends and raises her skirt, revealing a revolver
strapped to her thigh.

                    ELLIOT (CONT'D)
          Ah.

                    VILMA
          That's nothing. Look what I pack up
          here.

She raises her skirt all the way to reveal her very male
endowment between her legs.

                    ELLIOT
          My god.

                    VILMA
          Yes, I know. But keeping to the
          subject at hand for the moment, you
          do need real security around here.

                    ELLIOT
          And you're real security?

                    VILMA
          Ok, I may be a grandfather --

                    ELLIOT
          You're a grandfather?

                    VILMA
          I married young, the night before I
          shipped out with the marines.

                    ELLIOT
          You're a marine?

                    VILMA
          Semper fi, you little prick.
          Sergeant, Korea..

                    ELLIOT
          No kidding.

Vilma searches around in her purse, fishes out an old photo,
Vilma in a prior life, in uniform, next to another soldier.

                    VILMA
          That's me with the cigar. That one -
          - he was the love of my life.
                    (MORE)

                    VILMA (CONT'D)
Killed. Sniper. I went out on
patrol, found the Chinese pissant
who did it, and broke his neck with
my own hands.

                    ELLIOT
My God!

                    VILMA
Actually, I made that last part up.
But I would of if I'd gotten a hold
of the sonofabitch, and
          (flexing his arm muscles --
          huge)
I'd do it today if I found him.

                    ELLIOT
Vilma? You're hired.

They shake hands.

                    ELLIOT (CONT'D)
Do you need some kind of uniform?

                    VILMA
Oh, I've got uniforms!

65   EXT. EL MONACO MOTEL -- NEXT TO BARN -- DAY   65

Elliot, wearing a suit and tie, paces behind his cabin. He
looks up to see Michael and a beautiful young woman both
riding toward him on horses. Michael dismounts.

                    MICHAEL
She's a beautiful ride. Great way
to commute to Max's.

He leads the horses away. The young woman pauses.

                    YOUNG WOMAN
That's a nice suit.

                    ELLIOT
For the press. Conference.

                    YOUNG WOMAN
Sure....You ok?

                    ELLIOT
I'm a little...nervous.

                    YOUNG WOMAN
              (smiling, taking out from
               her sleeve a huge joint)
          I've got just the thing.

She lights it up, takes a long drag, offers it to Elliot.

                    ELLIOT
          Ah, you know, maybe not, I'm
          actually feeling a little nauseous.

                    YOUNG WOMAN
          Hey, grass is the perfect cure for
          nausea!

                    ELLIOT
          Really?

                    YOUNG WOMAN
          Seriously.

                    ELLIOT
          Oh.

Elliot takes a small puff.

                    ELLIOT (CONT'D)
          Hmmm.

                    YOUNG WOMAN
          Yeah.

                    ELLIOT
              (slight wheeze)
          Good shit.

Elliot takes another, bigger drag.

He coughs out a cloud of smoke.

                    YOUNG WOMAN
          Very good shit!

66   INT. EL MONACO BARN -- DAY   66

Fifteen or so journalists, microphones, notepads and pens. A
couple of tv cameras. In the back, a bunch of the Woodstock
people. Don is finishing his introduction.

                    DON
          ...and in these next few days
          before the concert we'll also
          provide daily briefings and we're
          all here to provide any follow up,
          but without further ado, here is
          Mr. Elliot Tiber, the proprietor of
          the El Monaco, President of the
          Bethel Chamber of Commerce, and a
          community liaison for Woodstock
          Ventures. Mr. Tiber.

And now we see Elliot approach the podium, an imperceptible
grin on his face.

                    ELLIOT
             (slowwwly)
          Good afternoon, ladies and
          gentlemen of the press.

So far, he's surprisingly together. Perhaps he's not stoned
after all.

Immediately, the questions start coming.

                    JOURNALIST 1
          Do you have a legal permit to
          conduct a concert in White Lake?

                    ELLIOT
          There will be a music and arts
          festival held here on August
          fifteen, sixteen, and seventeen,
          part of my ongoing yearly music and
          arts festivals that have made White
          Lake the truly international
          cultural center that it is. As
          evidenced by the fact that you
          wonderful ladies and gentlemen of
          the press are here to report on it.
          I have been proud to be the
          artistic director of the festival
          in its prior incarnations, and I
          hope that --

                    JOURNALIST 1
          Yes, but do you have a legal permit
          for the concert?

                    ELLIOT
             (pause)
          Of course. Need I remind you, I am
          the president.
                    (MORE)

ELLIOT (CONT'D)
The president, of the Bethel
Chamber of Commerce. Would a
leading civic leader such as myself
break his own laws? That doesn't
make sense.

JOURNALIST 2
Do you realize that the police are
now estimating that perhaps as many
as 100,000 people will attend the
concert? What will your people here
in White Lake think of 100,000
hippies and what they will do to
the town?

ELLIOT
My people? You say my people?
Native White Lakians cannot be
considered people -- mine or anyone
else's.

A slight wave of discomfort ripples through the room, as the
journalists start talking over each other.

JOURNALIST 2
Can you tell us something about
these free programs for the local
community happening this week?

JOURNALIST 3
Will there be a cap on the number
of tickets sold? How will you deal
with people showing up without
tickets?

Elliot is having a hard time hearing the questions.

ELLIOT
Ah. You are asking about freedom.
The very essence of the enterprise,
of all enterprise, especially free
enterprise. And freedom is often
considered to be, as you know, just
another word for...for being free.
Therefore, there will be no
train...to freedom. Because Train
has already left the station. For
how can the music be free when the
people of White Lake are enchained?
That is the question. If one song
is not free than all songs are not
free. That's why we are going to
free all the songs in White Lake.

Everyone is taking notes.

                    JOURNALIST 1
               (to the journalist next to
                him)
          Any idea what the hell is going on
          here?

                                             JUMP TO:
Later, Michael pushes forward as the journalists exit. Elliot
stands rather dazed.

                    MICHAEL
               (a slight tinge of
                nervousness)
          Wow, Elliot. You stood strong up
          there. That freedom
          rap...yeah...that was heavy.

                    ELLIOT
          Thanks Michael. You smell good.
          Like an apple fritter.

                    MICHAEL
               (bummed)
          Far out.

67   INT. EL MONACO MOTEL -- BUNGALOW -- NIGHT   67

Elliot, snoring, sound asleep. We hold close on his face, as
it twitches slightly -- the sound of voices, cars honking,
singing: his dreams? Light occasionally flashes across his
face, as the voices grow more insistent, and his visage
becomes more agitated.

Suddenly, he bolts awake.

The voices continue. We realize they are coming from outside.
He gets up, throws on a robe, and slowly opens the door.

68   EXT. EL MONACO MOTEL -- NIGHT   68

He walks up the hill toward the road to a surreal scene -- a
moonlit traffic jam on the road in front of the motel, as
hordes of concertgoers slowly wend their way to Yasgar's
farm.

Jake, with a coat thrown over his pajamas, is out directing
traffic with a whistle in his mouth. He waves to Elliot; he's
clearly having a good time.

As Elliot reaches the road he calls out to one of the young
people.

>   ELLIOT
>   What's happening?

>   YOUNG MAN
>   Didn't you hear? It's free, man!
>   The concert's free!

Elliot turns, and realizes Vilma has come up, standing beside
him, a coffee mug in hand.

>   VILMA
>   (nodding toward Jake)
>   He's been out there almost two
>   hours already. He won't budge.

Vilma runs over to Jake, who already appears to have struck
up quite a rapport with Vilma. Elliot looks on as Vilma gets
him to drink some coffee.

69   INT. EL MONACO MOTEL BAR -- SUNRISE   69

The first rays of morning light are coming up through the
windows as Elliot and Vilma drink their coffees.

After a while, Vilma breaks the silence.

>   VILMA
>   Your dad says you're a painter.

>   ELLIOT
>   When did he say that?

>   VILMA
>   I had him give me a tour of the
>   property, get the lay of the land.
>   He talked a lot about you, about
>   Brooklyn. He showed me some of his
>   favorite places -- the oaks down by
>   the lake. Nice.

>   ELLIOT
>   Wait. Are you sure that was my dad?
>   Maybe it was somebody else's.

Vilma smiles.

                    ELLIOT (CONT'D)
          I mean, he doesn't have any
          favorite places here -- he hates
          it. And he doesn't talk.

                    VILMA
          I'm not saying it was a therapy
          session. We were just chatting.

                    ELLIOT
          Chatting -- his mind must be going.

                    VILMA
          Don't worry Elliot -- I'll keep an
          eye on him. If he starts to smile,
          or laugh, or anything suspicious
          like that, I'll let you know.

                    ELLIOT
          Yeah. You do that.

                    VILMA
             (getting up)
          In fact, I've got to collect your
          dad's bat -- we've got dawn patrol!

                    ELLIOT
          Vilma? Does my dad know, you know,
          what you are?

                    VILMA
             (pauses, leans over and
              gives a kiss on Elliot's
              forehead)
          Oh Elliot. I know what I am. That
          does make it easier for everyone
          else, doesn't it?

     Vilma is off.

70   INT. EL MONACO MOTEL -- WOODSTOCK OFFICES -- DAY   70

     Elliot is walking with Don through the crowded office -- a
     manic energy infuses the entire place, as some of the workers
     are packing up to move closer the concert site on the eve of
     its beginning.

                    DON
          After the concert, we've got tables
          set up near the barn. I understand
          your mother is preparing her
          specialty --

                    ELLIOT
          -- Cholent? Oh no.

                    DON
          And the Ladies Auxillary has made
          desserts. We just have to make sure
          someone rations them -- there's a
          lot of hungry kids out there!

                    ELLIOT
          Don...I just want to say...I have a
          feeling.

                    DON
          Feelings. Feelings are good!

And he's off. Elliot stands in the center of the room, in a
daze. We overhear Penny, John, and Joel nearby.

                    PENNY
          They don't really know where to put
          all the sunflower seeds.

                    JOEL
          How many sunflower seeds did they
          buy?

                    PENNY
          Uh, how many seeds can you get into
          the back of a triple-axle trailer
          truck?

Paul, the cute guy from the bar, waves to him from the other
side of the room. Elliot blushes imperceptibly and tries to
nonchalantly walk over to him.

                    ELLIOT
          Hey.

                    PAUL
          Hey.

                    ELLIOT
          Working hard...everybody's working
          hard.

                    PAUL
          Yeah, very...hard.

                    ELLIOT
          Yeah.

                         PAUL
          I'm helping organize moving
          everybody from here and the
          Horseshoe up to the site, all the
          trailers and everything. We're
          gonna miss this place.

                         ELLIOT
          Yeah, well, we'll keep some rooms
          here in case you guys need to crash
          or anything.

                         PAUL
          Far out.

From the other side, John Roberts regards Elliot.

                         JOEL
          Hey John. Isn't that the prick who
          told everyone the concert's free?

                         JOHN
          Considering we haven't managed to
          build a ticket booth yet, I can't
          really argue with him.

70A   (We again go to split screen montage, seeing archival   70A
         footage and images of the preparation of the festival as we
         overhear various conversations.)

                         MEL
          Your guy at the National Guard said
          he could pull two more copters for
          us, right?

                         STAN
          Who took my pizza? And who took my
          walkie-talkie? And ask Michael if
          Penny can borrow his horse -- how
          the hell is she gonna get up to the
          site by noon with that traffic?

Back to Joel and John:

                         STEVE COHEN
          Should be. One issue though. The
          big towers for the speakers --

                         JOHN
          -- they're not staying up?

                    CHIP
          No, they're good. Solid. It's just
          that if there's rain, and
          lightning, well, they might get a
          little....

                    JOHN
          A little...

                    CHIP
          ...electrical.

                    STEVE COHEN
          We're working on it.

                    JOEL
          Yeah, we don't want to fry too much
          of the audience.

                    JOHN
          That's a good point, Joel.

                    JOEL
          Thanks, John.

                    SAM
          Hell, it's August -- it's not gonna
          rain.

John and Joel trade very worried glances.

Additional dialogue unfolding in the background:

                    MEL
               (on the phone)
          Fuck the alfalfa...not literally.
          What the hell are you on? Get that
          tractor over to the south field,
          and then find what's-his-name, he's
          gotta round up those cows...Sheep?
          Well just keep 'em away from the
          helicoport. Yeah, that could be
          ugly.

                    CHIP
               (on the phone)
          Hold on. The guy with the telephone
          poles...He what? Where did he leave
          them? That crew from Saugerties can
          do it... Hanley will be here
          tonight and he'll tell you.

                    STAN
               (on phone)
          How many sunflower seeds are in a
          pound? How am I supposed to know?
          Remember -- rice, bananas, anything
          that'll keep 'em from shitting --
          I'm worried about our toilet
          numbers.

71   EXT. EL MONACO MOTEL -- FRONT LAWN AREA -- DAY   71

In the midst of the chaos all around the motel grounds, a
small makeshift stage has been set up, and folding chairs,
half-filled with conservative-looking families, are seated
facing it, as a local, lousy, high school band finishes its
set. The kids pump their fists in the air; the adults clap
politely.

Don takes the stage and stands in front of the mic as the
band clears.

Elliot stands back behind the audience.

                    DON
          Thank you, Hairy Pretzel. It's so
          great that you let us share your
          music with all your friends and
          parents here from White Lake. And
          now, we'd like to introduce the
          resident theater artists here at
          the El Monaco this summer, the
          Earthlight Players, who have
          updated Anton Chekhov's classic,
          Three Sisters, to a contemporary
          happening interpretation, and they
          would like now to share a part of
          that experience with you. The
          Earthlight Players.

The troupe climbs up on the stage, some in faux-Victorian
outfits, walking, some in animal-like costumes, crouching.

                    DEVON
          Artifice -- and imagination! Truth,
          and fiction! The players play! But
          you, the audience, you sit and
          judge.

                    PLAYERS
               (in unison)
          You sit and judge.

                    DEVON
          But the revolution requires -- the
          roles must be reversed -- the
          players are the judges -- your
          revery must end -- and your souls
          will be bared for all to see!
          Christ who died for you, not for me
          -- now WE are Christ, our nakedness
          will reveal your own!

With that, the actors race to the front of the stage and
begin to disrobe, all the while hurling invective at the
audience.

                    ACTORS
          Indecent legions of decency!
          Fascist pornographers! Racist war
          mongers! Republican cocksuckers!

The audience is at first stunned, and then quickly parents
begin to rise, gather their things, cover their children's
eyes, and race away. In the midst of the crowd, we see Billy,
loving every minute of it. He jumps up on the stage and
starts to take his own clothes off. Pandemonium.

Elliot watches it all. Dan has come up beside him. He stands
and watches his brother cavort on stage with the players.
Billy waves to them from the stage.

                    DAN
          You having fun, Elliot? You think
          this is funny?

                    ELLIOT
          Dan, I....

                    DAN
          It's killing me. That...that used
          to be my brother. Now look at him.

                    ELLIOT
          Maybe if you just let it happen...

                    DAN
          Go with the flow, huh? Like you?
          How many people around here know
          which way you flow, Elliot? You
          told your parents? Yeah, you know,
          you're as much of a hypocrite as I
          am.

He walks down toward the stage, shouting for his brother.

                         DAN (CONT'D)
               Billy! Billy! Come down here!

On stage, amid the chaos, the now-naked players are being
chased off by Sonia.

As Elliot walks back toward the main motel building, we now
see that the property is really filling up with various vans,
tents, etc., as people begin to pitch camp wherever and
however.

72   EXT. EL MONACO MOTEL -- DAY   72

The road in front of the motel is jammed with traffic.

Elliot is at the pool, holding a hose, filling it as a couple
of kids gerryrig buckets on ropes. Behind him is a freshly
painted sign: No Swimming, Peeing, Balling or Anything in the
Pool -- Fresh Drinking Water!

Elliot looks over to the main office building, as the door
flies open, and two shady looking men come running out,
followed by Vilma and Jake, both holding bats.

Vilma and Jake chase the men around the corner. As they pass
Elliot, they happily wave to him.

                         JAKE
                  (smiling as he runs)
               Hi Elli!

Elliot walks after them, but they're out of sight.

72A   EXT. EL MONACO MOTEL -- BEHIND MAIN BUILDING -- DAY   72A

Elliot rounds the corner, to discover, sitting under a tree,
an Indian swami, cross-legged, surrounded by a dozen or so
disciples, among whom are Marge and Annie from the chamber of
commerce. Their foreheads are daubed with red clay, and they
wave to Elliot ecstatically.

                         ANNIE
               Namaste Elliot!

He waves back.

As Elliot wanders through and back toward the motel, when he
practically bumps into Tisha. She's balancing a load of
blankets.

                              TISHA
                    Hey Elliot!

Elliot takes some of the blankets just as they are about to
slide to the ground.

                              ELLIOT
                    Here.

                              TISHA
                    Thanks.

                              ELLIOT
                    Where we going with these?

                              TISHA
                    The barn. Stan and your theater guy
                    have set up some medical
                    volunteers. The combination of bare
                    feet and the brown acid is --

                              ELLIOT
                    Real?

                              TISHA
                    Very. We're grabbing everything we
                    can. Hope it's ok -- your mom gave
                    me these blankets.

                              ELLIOT
                    My mom? Gave?

                              TISHA
                    Yeah. She's cool.

Tisha and Elliot drop the blankets on a pile as volunteers
sort and carry supplies.

Across the lawn, a food delivery truck is pulling up. Elliot
sees Jake run up to it, and he goes to join his father.

72B   EXT. EL MONACO MOTEL -- DAY -- CONT.   72B

As the driver opens the back of the truck, Jake pulls up a
hand truck.

                              ELLIOT
                    Hey, Dad. Let me do that.

                              JAKE
                    Thanks. I can't believe he got
                    through.

The driver starts stacking boxes.

Suddenly they hear a shout from someone standing by the pool.

>   GUY AT MOTEL
>   Hey, look! Food!

>   PEOPLE
>   (ad lib)
>   Food! Food!

Suddenly, almost from nowhere, a mob descends toward the truck. Jake starts grabbing boxes and tries to make a run for it to the office, but he stumbles and the boxes go flying.

Elliot helps pick his father up, as Vilma arrives, baseball bat in hand, trying to stave off the crowd, some of whom have carted off some of the boxes. One is even open, and people start stuffing themselves with hot dog buns.

>   VILMA
>   Back off, everyone.

>   GUY AT MOTEL
>   Hey man, we're hungry!

>   PEOPLE
>   It's not fair! Feed the people!

Just as things are about to turn ugly, a young guy jumps up on the back of the truck, guitar in hand.

>   SINGER
>   Hey people! Hey! Maybe if we let
>   the man unload in peace, the big
>   lady won't hurt anyone, and maybe
>   we can all share together if we get
>   organized and help each other.

>   JAKE
>   That's right.

>   SINGER
>   Far out!

He tunes his guitar, and then launches into an almost-on-key version of a folk standard. The crowd settles as Jake, Vilma and Elliot commence unloading the truck again. Some of the kids help out.

73   INT. EL MONACO MOTEL -- BACK ROOM -- DAY   73

In the back room, Sonia is parked in front of the tv.

>   TV REPORTER
>   That's right. The New York State
>   Thruway has been backed up all the
>   way from the George Washington
>   Bridge to the Catskills exits, and
>   from there it's basically a parking
>   lot. Police are now planning to put
>   into effect a first-ever emergency
>   closing of the entire thruway --

Elliot comes in.

>   ELLIOT
>   Mom, you ok?

>   SONIA
>   The *nish-gute* -- evil -- you see
>   the chicken-legs on some of these
>   hairy people? *Nish-gute*!

>   ELLIOT
>   They're kids, not evil spirits.

>   SONIA
>   You don't know. They've made all
>   the roads one way now, Elli. One
>   way just to Max's. God forbid, what
>   if your father should have a heart
>   attack from all this running
>   around, he couldn't get to the
>   hospital.

>   ELLIOT
>   You really are worried about him,
>   aren't you?

>   SONIA
>   Him? It's you who brought this --
>   How will you live with the guilt?

74   INT. EL MONACO MOTEL -- BAR AREA -- NIGHT   74

The place is hopping. Two guitar players and a couple of
drummers sit up front, and young people are dancing, smoking,
rapping all over. Black light posters have been put up. New
faces are helping Elliot out at the bar.

To one side, Vilma, Jake, and a middle-aged lesbian couple sit talking. Jake says something and the group laughs appreciatively.

Jake and Vilma join Elliot at the bar.

> ELLIOT
> How you doing Dad?

> JAKE
> How should I be doing? I haven't slept in three days, my hip is killing me, the beer is warm.

> ELLIOT
> So...you're good.

> JAKE
> Yeah. I'm good. Hand me that bottle.
> (to Vilma)
> Another?

> VILMA
> I thought you'd never ask.

Jake goes back to his corner.

> VILMA (CONT'D)
> (to Elliot)
> Hey kid, how are you doing?

> ELLIOT
> I haven't slept in three days, the beer is warm, and, I'm actually not making this up, my hip kind of aches.

> VILMA
> So...you're good!

Vilma goes back to join Jack and a group of older folks. The beat of the music picks up and the dancing becomes more sensual.

Elliot, looking to collect empties, gets pulled into a dance by two girls. The crowd starts to clap.

> CROWD
> (ad lib)
> Do it, Elliot! Get into the groove.

He is, of course, a terrible dancer. But he gamely gives it a shot.

One of the girls sidles up to him and kisses him. Cheers. He
gently pulls away. Others join the intimate dance. As Elliot
turns to get back to the bar, he's pulled into another kiss --
with Paul, the cute construction guy from earlier. Even more
cheers. Paul pulls back, a big smile on his face. Elliot
stands stunned for a second, then goes back for another kiss.
Even more cheers.

When he pulls back again, he looks over at the table where
his father was sitting, but Jake is no longer there.

75   OMITTED   75

76   EXT. ROAD IN FRONT OF EL MONACO MOTEL -- DAY   76

A total logjam of kids attempting to make their way to the
concert now. Among them, a news reporter standing in front of
the camera, mic in hand.

                    NEWS REPORTER
              State authorities now estimate that
              perhaps half a million kids have
              already made it to the White Lake
              area, and there's another million
              trying to get there who just will
              never make it, putting upstate
              communities in an uproar at this
              major hippie invasion.

Elliot walks up to the intersection, to discover a group of
locals, all holding signs ("By Order of Bethel Town Council,
The concert is Cancelled" "This is an unlawful Aseembly, You
are Subject to Arrest"), trying to block the way to the
concert. No one pays attention to them, as the huge crows
just simply walks around. Bob is among the group.

                    ELLIOT
              Bob, what's this all about?

                    BOB
              We got the permit pulled, you
              idiot, we're shutting this thing
              down!

                    ELLIOT
              But...there's half a million people
              over at Max's, how do you think
              they're going to react?

                    BOB
          That's the same thing the cops said
          --

                    CAROL
          -- Before they laughed at us, as if
          we were children!

                    BOB
          So we're doing it ourselves.

                    ELLIOT
          Right.

Elliot sees, back at the motel, his father and Vilma again
running with baseball bats in hand.

He takes off after them as they head toward the lake.

77   EXT. EL MONACO MOTEL -- LAKEFRONT -- DAY   77

Elliot arrives to see Vilma and Jake chasing into the water a
small group of local toughs.

Jake is winded but beaming.

                    JAKE
          You should have seen us, Elli.

                    VILMA
          They were about to spray paint
          Georgette's bus.

                    JAKE
          Vilma got there first. Got a hold
          of one. I had my tar ready, landed
          a nice warm ball of tar right on
          his face!

                    VILMA
          They all started running after
          that!

Vilma and Jake high five.

Jake catches his breath again, looks over the lake. There are
small groups of people bathing and swimming.

                    JAKE
          This is where we rinse the sheets.
          There's some nice bushes here.

                    ELLIOT
          Yeah, dad.

A moment of peace as they stand there, overlooking the lake,
taking it in.

And then, faintly at first, a strange electronic sound can be
heard from far off, and then he muffled sounds of an
amplified voice.

                    JAKE
          Can you hear that?

                    ELLIOT
          It's starting.

The sounds begin to take on a rhythmic quality, the sound of
hundreds of thousands of hands clapping, keeping time. It's
distant, but becoming a little bit more distinct, as the
sounds float over the lakewater. Jake and Vilma begin to nod
their heads slightly in time with the beat, as we begin
barely to hear a voice over the clapping....

"Hey look yonder, what's that you see? Marching to the fields
of Concord..."

                    JAKE
          Elli.

                    ELLIOT
          What?

                    JAKE
          You should go. To Max's. We can
          take care of things here. Go, see
          this thing.

                    VILMA
          Go see what the center of the
          universe looks like.

                    ELLIOT
          Sure. Yeah.

He gives his dad a quick, slightly awkward hug.

                    ELLIOT (CONT'D)
          Thanks. I'll be back soon!

78   EXT. ROAD IN FRONT OF EL MONACO MOTEL -- DAY   78

Elliot gets to the road, stands next to a state trooper who's
been helping direct traffic. The trooper has a flower in his
helmet.

                    ELLIOT
          Wow.

                    TROOPER
          Bet you thought you were gonna just
          drive right up to the thing, huh?

                    ELLIOT
          Actually, that's my motel right
          there.

                    TROOPER
          The El Monaco, huh? So you're the
          guy they're all blaming for
          bringing all this here. Governor
          just declared the whole county a
          disaster area.

                    ELLIOT
          Yeah, it's a disaster -- I'm the
          disaster guy -- officially!

                    TROOPER
          No kiddin'. I was just looking
          forward to coming up here and
          clubbing a bunch of hippies over
          the head. I must be gettin' high
          off the fumes, but instead, I don't
          know --

At that moment, a group of kids walks by -- one of them
flashes the peace sign.

                    YOUNG MAN
          Peace man!

The trooper flashes a peace sign back.

                    TROOPER
          You see what I mean?

                    ELLIOT
          Groovy. I think I'll head over
          there and check it all out.

                         TROOPER
               On foot? It'll take you all
               afternoon with this crowd. Here.

                                                    CUT TO:

79   EXT. ROAD IN FRONT OF MOTEL -- DAY   79

          Elliot, his arms around the trooper, sitting on the back of
          the trooper's chopper, as the trooper guides it through the
          crowds on the road, occasionally flipping on his siren.

79A   EXT. ROUTE 17B -- DAY   79A

          In a long tracking shot reminiscent of the famous traffic jam
          shot from Godard's *Weekend*, we follow along with Elliot and
          the trooper as they make their way, with stops and starts,
          through the surreal scene. But instead of *Weekend*'s
          dystopian vision, we'll discover a panoply of vignettes and
          scenes of the Woodstock nation, 1969:

          Prayer circles,

          jam sessions,

          cook-outs,

          A man and woman in shorts and sandals dancing; he wearing a
          Nixon mask and she a Kissinger mask;

          A stalled truck filled with port-o-potties, young people
          perched atop them passing around water-pipes;

          A 16mm film crew, interviewing a young couple;

          A couple of stray cows, garlanded with flowers;

          A young couple, fully clothed, but clearly "doing it on the
          road" as people pass by;

          Gaggles of naked children, etc.

          After a long stretch, the trooper gets a call on his walkie-
          talkie and responds.

                         TROOPER
               Roger that. (To Elliot) Sorry, I've
               got to head back to town. You're
               gonna have to make it on your own
               from here on.

Elliot climbs off.

                    ELLIOT
          Thanks for the lift!

Elliot commences to walk with the crowd for a while, but he's getting a bit hot and tired -- it's slow going. We hear in the distance the thumping of the speakers from the concert throughout.

Elliot looks into the woods by the road and sees various encampments. He wanders in.

80   EXT. WOODS BY THE ROAD -- CONT.   80

Here are makeshift tents and lean-tos, groups of young people sitting, tripping, hanging out. Elliot wanders through the encampment.

Someone has attached a sign to one of the trees, with an arrow pointing to "Groovy Way." Elliot follows it into the grove.

He joins a small stream of young people to discover a makeshift drug supermarket in the woods.

                    DEALER
          Panamanian red, Mexican gold,
          temple balls, Sandoz, Sunshine...

He passes by some booths where lefties of all stripes are handing out flyers;

A free food booth run by the Hog Farmers dishing out gruel;

A section of the fence into the concert grounds being pulled down and a bunch of young guys pushing through it.

A "trip tent" run by Abbie Hoffman's yippies; Elliot sees Billy helping out, joined by a bunch of other Vietnam Vets, all in their rag tag uniforms -- Billy looks up and waves to him.

                    BILLY
          Hey Elliot. Look who I found --
          Fuckin' Loony Lenny from Charlie
          Company!

He goes back to comfort a young kid freaking out;

Elliot moves on, finally coming across a psychedelically-painted vw van parked under a tree.

Sitting in the open van door are a beautiful young hippie
couple. The back of the van's floor is a big mattress covered
with silks and patterned blankets -- a veritable love bug.

                    GUY
          Hey, man. You look thirsty.

                    ELLIOT
          I am.

The girl pours Elliot a glass from a jug.

                    ELLIOT (CONT'D)
          Thanks. Have you been to the
          festival yet?

                    GUY
          We're cool. We'll get there again.

                    GIRL
          We got to the top of the hill,
          looked down at the sea, and the
          tiny little people on the stage
          with their waves of tiny electric
          voices.

                    GUY
          Like ants making thunder. It was
          cool. But you couldn't really tell
          who was jamming down there.

                    GIRL
          And we left our trip in the car.

                    GUY
          And the shit they're passing around
          down there -- not quality.

                    GIRL
          Ours is beautiful.

                    ELLIOT
          I see the California plates...is
          that where you're from?

                    GIRL
          There, and New Mexico --

                    GUY
          -- and Oregon...

                    ELLIOT
          You're from everywhere.

                    GIRL
          We're from everywhere! You're from
          everywhere!

                    ELLIOT
          I'm from here.

They start laughing.

                    GUY
          You're from here, right now, from
          here, here's where you're from --
          you're from here, man!

                    GIRL
          That's so cool!

                    ELLIOT
          I guess so.

                    GUY
          No man, you're amazingly from here!

                    ELLIOT
          You're right. I never really
          thought about ...being....from
          ....here, before, and going --
          here?

We now see that the girl's holding a blotter sheet of acid in
her hand.

                    GIRL
          On a trip with us!

                    ELLIOT
          To California?

                    GUY
          Here man -- take a ride to here and
          now.

The girl takes a tab, and gently places it on the guy's
tongue. Then offers one to Elliot.

                    GIRL
          Eight miles high.

                    ELLIOT
          I'm actually a little afraid of
          heights....Well, what the heck!

She smiles. Then leans over. He opens his mouth and she
places the tab on his tongue, then another on her own.

> GUY
> Hey, come on in and sit.

Later:

81   INT. VAN -- DAY   81

Elliot sits awkwardly between the two of them. A soft light
bathes them through the van's window's shades. Elliot looks a
little bored, gazing at all the posters and designs plastered
on the ceiling and walls: Fillmore posters, R. Crumb-like
comic images, "Eastern" designs.

> ELLIOT
> So...

> GUY
> Yeah...

> ELLIOT
> You sure that was acid? I didn't
> really taste like any --

> GIRL
> It just takes a while. Hey, let's
> listen to some of our own sounds.

There's a sound system in the front. The guy puts on a trippy
album -- Love, or The Incredible String Band.

Elliot pretends to relax to the beat, but clearly is not yet
feeling anything and starting to get a wee bit antsy. Slowly,
at first imperceptibly, our perception of the music begins to
change, and we can see from Elliot's face that the acid is
starting to kick in.

His pov: The posters and designs start to move a little,
their colors deepening. He breaks into a sweat, and starts to
scratch himself a bit.

> ELLIOT
> (looking at his arm
> closely)
> That's a funny spider.

He leans back, closes, then opens, his eyes, starting to feel
himself losing some boundaries.

                    ELLIOT (CONT'D)
          What...what is that?

                    GIRL
          It's ok. Just breathe.

Elliot leans back. Takes deep breaths. The music begins to
enfold around him.

His pov: the girl's beatific smile. He turns: on his other
side, the guy, smiling too. Elliot looks down: each of them
begins to touch him.

81A   EXT. VAN -- DAY   81A

        As the trip commences...

82   INT. VAN -- DAY   82

        Acid trip sequence -- Elliot and his two companions tripping,
        touching each other, laughing.

        One possible visual reference for this sequence is Bob
        Rafelson's "Head" -- there might be flashes of images from
        Woodstock, Vietnam, etc.; the visual treatment might be
        derived and fairly faithful to sixties representations of the
        drug experience (this will be more "optical" than "digital"
        in look and feel). We will cue off the posters and designs in
        the van for the trip images.

        Later:

83   INT./EXT. VAN -- NIGHT   83

        Elliot lies awake, lying between his two companions -- and
        perhaps a third or fourth...

        We hear the beat of the concert from afar, as a faint
        moonlight filters into the van.

        He gingerly rises; his shirt is off, but his pants are still
        on. He grabs the closest shirt and gently opens the van door.
        The girl wakes up as he does so, and smiles at him. She wraps
        a shawl around herself and follows him out.

84   EXT. VAN -- NIGHT   84

     Elliot puts on the clothes as she comes up behind him. There
     are people sleeping all around them, in sleeping bags on the
     ground, a few tents pitched, others asleep in their cars.

                         GIRL
               Hey. Let's go down to the ocean.
               Let's go swim.

     Elliot nods. They wander through the encampment -- people
     gathered around fire pits, sitting in clusters.

     They walk up an incline, as the crowd thickens.

     The music grows in intensity and clarity -- it's Ravi
     Shankhar on sitar, giving way to a hypnotic tabla solo, which
     then morphs into the whole ensemble playing a transcendent
     raga.

     As Elliot and the girl crest the top of the hill, they join a
     crowd standing and swaying to the music. In the darkness
     below them, one can sense a vast expanse of a half-million
     people, swaying and dancing, flickering lights among them; at
     the bottom of the meadow, far, far below, a tiny dot of light
     illuminates what we can barely sense is the stage.

     Elliot and the girl raise their arms and join the crowd atop
     the hill, smiling, swirling and dancing, tears streaming down
     their faces.

85   EXT. ROAD -- DAWN   85

     Elliot groggily walks back in the pale light just before
     sunrise-- barefoot and wearing a Mexican peasant shirt --
     signs of life barely stirring all around.

85A   EXT. BARN - DAWN   85A

     By the barn, he comes across Vilma, in a mud-splattered
     dress, a two-day growth of beard on his face but still traces
     of lipstick on his mouth, helping four elderly local ladies,
     all working together packing boxes of sandwiches onto a pick-
     up.

     Elliot looks down at Vilma's feet, now shod in old combat
     boots.

                VILMA
Hi Elliot. Meet the ladies from St
Paul's in Liberty. They made 5,0000
sandwiches!

             ST PAUL LADY
Oh Vilma, don't exaggerate. We made
4,000.

                VILMA
What do you think of that?

                ELLIOT
     (more or less comatose)
Mmrrrr.

Vilma laughs and goes back to work as Elliot stumbles away.

86   EXT. EL MONACO MOTEL -- FRONT LAWN AREA - DAY   86

Elliot's parents come out of the office as he arrives. His
father is carrying a huge stack of laundry.

                SONIA
My God! Look at him! Where have you
been all day and night?

                JAKE
How was the concert?

                ELLIOT
Well, I met some friends on the way
there, and, uh, I think it was
great -- it was great.

Jake lets it sink in. He's impressed.

                JAKE
Hmmm.

                SONIA
Are you hungry?

                ELLIOT
Yeah. I'm starving.

87   INT. EL MONACO MOTEL -- FRONT OFFICE -- DAY   87

Elliot and his parents sit down to eat pancakes. The place is
abuzz with activity.

                    ELLIOT
          So I was thinking, when this is
          over --

                    SONIA
          What a mess! It'll take months to
          clean up.

                    ELLIOT
          But we can keep some of these new
          people on, right? We can afford the
          help now. And with the place paid
          off, maybe it's time you thought
          about some permanent staff, people
          to help you run the place, make
          some improvements.

                    SONIA
          What are you talking about? That's
          why we have you!

She gives Elliot a look over.

                    ELLIOT
          I'm just saying, I was thinking,
          when this is over, with all the
          money now, I could take a trip --

                    SONIA
          And where did you get those
          pyjamas? You're not going anywhere
          dressed like that!

Vilma and a celebratory crowd of Woodstockers enters; Vilma
holds a tray.

                    VILMA
          We've made brownies! Wonderful
          brownies! Some very special
          brownies! Elliot?

                    ELLIOT
          We'll take a pass.

Vilma and company move on, passing out brownies to the
assembled.

                    SONIA
          You see, Jake? That's just like
          him. He doesn't want dessert, but
          does he think to ask his mother?

                    ELLIOT
                (getting up)
        You know what? That's enough. You
        know, I'm the only one here, out of
        hundreds and hundreds and hundreds
        of thousands of people, who's
        having breakfast with his parents!
        Do you think Janis Joplin's mom is
        backstage telling her to tuck her,
        I don't know, her whiskey bottle
        into her pocket, or something? Or
        Jimi Hendrix's mom is telling him
        to wash his hair? I'm just going to
        go to Max's and enjoy myself -- and
        you know what? Go ahead! I'd love
        to see you eat one of those
        brownies -- you should have two!

His parents are in shock.

He walks out. Sonia is about to say something, but Jake
interrupts her.

                    SONIA
        Elli!

                    JAKE
        Leave the boy.

88   EXT. EL MONACO MOTEL -- DAY   88

Elliot walks toward the road. Michael Lang rides up to him on
a shiny motorcycle. A 16mm camera crew lopes along beside
him, filming him.

                    ELLIOT
        Hey Mike. I hear all the fences got
        torn down, and no one's buying
        tickets.

                    MICHAEL
        Yeah, the whole ticket thing was
        getting to be a real drag, as you
        knew. (quoting Elliot) "You freed
        all the songs in White Lake, Elli!"

                    ELLIOT
        Sorry about that...So how are you
        going to pay for everything?
        Where's the money going to come
        from?

                    MICHAEL
          You always worry, don't you, Elli?
          Look up in the sky, man, the money
          will fall from the sky!

He rides off. Elliot looks after him, and then up at the sky:
Clouds.

John and Joel come running up as Michael rides away, Stan
behind them.

                    JOHN
          There he goes, in full Technicolor.

                    JOEL
               (to Stan)
          Get someone on a donkey with a
          lasso to corral that guy and get
          him back here -- The Who won't go
          on unless we pay cash!

                    JOHN
          And if the Who doesn't go on...

                    JOEL
          The What hits the fan.

Elliot watches them jog back to the offices, then starts
walking toward the road. As he does, he pauses: a gaggle of
Jewish kids are staring at him from Polonsky's. He flashes
them a peace sign. Solemnly, the all raise their hands and
give him a peace sign back.

89   EXT. ROAD - DAY   89

          Elliot marches along with the crowd, but the sky has already
          turned overcast and the wind has picked up.

          A flash of lightning, and then the crackle of thunder.

          The rain begins, and in an instant it's coming down in
          buckets. People begin to scatter and seek shelter, others
          keep marching on toward the concert.

89A   EXT. ROAD NEXT TO CORNFIELD - DAY   89A

          The rain, if possible, has gotten even worse. Elliot trudges
          on. A car door opens.

                    PARKED HIPPIE
          Hey man, want some shelter from the
          rain?

                    ELLIOT
          No thanks. I took that trip
          already!

                    PARKED HIPPIE
          Far out.

As Elliot walks on, he's joined by Billy, who marches happily
alongside him.

Laughing, they put their arms around each other and keep
walking in the rain.

89B   EXT. MUDDY HILL - DAY   89B

The rain has stopped, and the road has turned into a muddy
river. Elliot and Billy trudge on. Billy suddenly stops at
the bottom of a hill.

                    BILLY
          Oh man, I remember this hill.

                    ELLIOT
          You mean, remember remember or like
          Vietnam flashback remember?

                    BILLY
          Remember remember, man. Homecoming.
          Senior year. We fuckin massacred
          Monticello. I caught like three
          touchdown passes. Rum and cokes.
          And we fuckin' tipped three of
          Yasgar's cows, right up there --
          and then Shirley Livingstone, man,
          right up there, at the top of that
          hill --

                    ELLIOT
          Wait a second.

Elliot studies Billy's face, stunned.

                    ELLIOT (CONT'D)
          Amazing...that was you --

                    BILLY
          Was...is,...

                    ELLIOT
          And that's THE Shirley Livingstone,
          the one who works at the animal
          hospital?

                    BILLY
                (quiet)
          We were engaged, man.

He starts walking up the hill.

                    BILLY (CONT'D)
          C'mon man, I love this fuckin'
          hill!

Around them, people have begun to use the hill as a mudslide,
whizzing down on their backs. One of the sliders almost
crashes into Elliot -- he crankily moves aside, almost
slipping.

                    ELLIOT
          Hey, watch it.

But as he takes his next step, he starts to slide backward,
and in spite of his and Billy's frantic efforts to stay
erect, they tilt over and fall in the mud.

They get up, take another step, and fall over again, falling
into a couple of other festgoers, who also tumble.

They all lie together in the mud, starting to laugh
hysterically.

Elliot scoops up some mud and throws it at the others. They
throw mud back. And soon its a full-fledged mud fight on the
road.

Elliot and Billy fall again. This time they just lie on their
backs, laughing. It's hard to say if Billy is crying, too.

                    BILLY
          I love this hill!

                    ELLIOT
          We love this hill!

90   EXT. EL MONACO MOTEL -- NIGHT   90

It's raining again as a waterlogged and muddy Elliot walks
back. Vilma is sitting under the awning.

> VILMA
> The prodigal son is back!

> ELLIOT
> Well, you know, I didn't quite, you
> know, go.

Vilma puts his arm around Elliot.

> VILMA
> Got it. I'm happy to see you. And I
> want to introduce you to some very
> groovy people. Come with me.

91   EXT. EL MONACO MOTEL - FRONT OFFICE - BACK PORCH - NIGHT   91

Vilma leads Elliot into the office. We stay close on Elliot's
face as he stops up short; we hear hysterical laughter.

> ELLIOT
> You gave them the hash brownies?

> VILMA
> They told me you said they should!

> ELLIOT
> How many?

> VILMA
> Four each.

We now see Elliot's pov: his parents, dancing, laughing,
totally stoned.

They spot him.

> SONIA
> Eliyahu! My baby!

> JAKE
> Her baby!

He cracks up anew at this.

> ELLIOT
> (stage whisper)
> Oh my God.

They come running up to him and give him huge hugs.

> SONIA
> Elli! My baby boy! My filthy baby
> boy! Give mamma some of that dirt!

> JAKE
> And save some for me!

At first Elliot is horrified. But then he looks at Vilma, who
shrugs and smiles, and, though still freaked out, he gives
his parents a hug back.

Jake and Sonia, laughing, begin dancing again. Some passersby
join them. Even Elliot joins in a bit.

92   OMITTED   92

93   INT. EL MONACO MOTEL -- FRONT OFFICE -- NIGHT   93

Sonia and Jake, soaking wet, burst into the front office and
find their way to the back room, followed by Elliot.

Elliot pauses by the front door, trying to take in just what
happened.

He walks into the back room.

> ELLIOT
> Ma --

He sees his parents, each collapsed in a separate chair,
sound asleep.

He goes to the closet, gets a sweater and a blanket, tucks
his parents in as best he can, and leaves.

94   INT. EL MONACO MOTEL -- ELLIOT'S BUNGALOW -- NIGHT   94

Elliot takes a shower.

He dries off, gets dressed.

There's a knock on the door. He opens the door. It's Dan.

> DAN
> Elliot. Can I come in?

> ELLIOT
> Sure, I guess.

Dan closes the door behind him. He seems a bit frantic.

>   ELLIOT (CONT'D)
>   What is it?

Dan holds out an envelope to Elliot.

>   DAN
>   Could you...when you see
>   Billy...could you give this to him
>   for me?

>   ELLIOT
>   Why don't you give it to him
>   yourself?

>   DAN
>   It's a little complicated -- I'm
>   leaving town for a while. Carol
>   threw me out. I tried to throw her
>   out but she threw me out first. You
>   know?

>   ELLIOT
>   What happened?

>   DAN
>   She couldn't get to work. The
>   traffic and all. Came back, and
>   found me --

>   ELLIOT
>   Ah, you were being naughty.

>   DAN
>   Not only that, they were...

>   ELLIOT
>   They?

>   DAN
>   They were both...negroes.

Elliot let's out a laugh.

>   DAN (CONT'D)
>   It's not funny. (holding his hands
>   out from his head) They had hair,
>   out to here. So she comes in.
>   (MORE)

                    DAN (CONT'D)
          Ok, I was thinking, I have to think
          fast here, I don't know what I was
          thinking, so I say, "Hey hon, you
          want to join?" And you know what
          she says?

                    ELLIOT
          No?

                    DAN
          "Yes!" She says yes! Carol! Married
          five years and that's what she'd
          say at a time like that!

                    ELLIOT
          So that's why you tried to throw
          her out?

                    DAN
          Not just. But it was some fight.
          Shit.
               (he thinks for a moment)
          You know, you owe me, Elliot. It's
          all your fault. You brought 'em all
          here!

Elliot doesn't take the bait.

                    ELLIOT
          I'll give this to Billy when I see
          him. It was good of you to think of
          him.

Dan nods, opens the door.

                    DAN
          Yeah. He's a good kid.

95   EXT. ROAD IN FRONT OF EL MONACO MOTEL -- DAY   95

The last morning, and now the sea of humanity -- bedraggled,
exhausted, coming down - is flowing in the opposite
direction.

There is trash and debris everywhere.

95A INT. ELLIOT'S BUNGALOW -- MORNING   95A

Elliot yawns, awakening.

He looks over: lying next to him, sound asleep, is Paul.

Elliot quietly gets up and puts on some clothes.

96   INT. EL MONACO MOTEL -- FRONT OFFICE -- DAY   96

Elliot enters the motel office and walks to the back room.

There he finds his father standing, looking down upon his
sleeping mother -- although instead of being tucked into the
rocking chair she's curled up on the floor half-way in the
utility closet, cradling stacks of money she had hid under a
floorboard that has now been pried up.

                    ELLIOT
          Dad --

                    JAKE
               (half whisper)
          Shhh -- she's still sleeping.

                    ELLIOT
               (whispering)
          Still? It's practically noon. And
          how long have you been standing
          here like this?

                    JAKE
          I don't know. She got up in her
          sleep, walked over there, and...

                    ELLIOT
          What's with... the money? We've
          been depositing everything that's
          come in this week -- where did all
          that come from?

Sonia stirs awake, hearing their voices. She opens her eyes,
sees them, sees the money, and then, in a panic, tries to
cover it up.

                    ELLIOT (CONT'D)
          Mom, what the hell?

                    SONIA
          Don't come near me you two!

                    ELLIOT
          But what --

                    SONIA
          -- It's mine! It's my savings. For
          twenty years, my savings!

                ELLIOT
        Jesus, how much have you got there?

                SONIA
        None of your business....$97,000.

                ELLIOT
        $97,000! Dad, did you know about
        this?

                JAKE
        You think she'd tell me?

                ELLIOT
        Wait a sec. You'd of let the bank
        foreclose? Let me put all my
        earnings into this place...? And
        you...?

                JAKE
          (putting his hand on
          Elliot's arm)
        Elli. What does it matter? We're
        rich now.

He pats Elliot's arm, and walks slowly out. Elliot is near
tears.

Sonia hastily puts the bills back under the floorboard, and
turns back to Elliot.

She can barely speak, on the verge of shameful tears.

                SONIA
        Elli, I was scared.

Elliot just looks at her, with a dawning compassion.

                ELLIOT
        Oh, mom.

Silence.

                SONIA
          (leaving, quietly)
        I've got to fix your father his
        lunch.

She walks out. He stands and stares at the door. He walks
out, too.

97   EXT. EL MONACO MOTEL -- FRONT OFFICE -- DAY   97

Elliot stands in front of the office, takes a deep breath.
Billy is sitting next to the door. They smile at each other.

                    BILLY
          Fuck.

Elliot takes this in, nodding, sits, and puts his arm around
Billy.

                    BILLY (CONT'D)
          You ok there bro?

                    ELLIOT
          Me? Yeah. No...Um, you ever look
          back on your life, and think,
          um....Fuck.

                    BILLY
          Yeah! Sure. But then, fuck.

                    ELLIOT
          Hey, I almost forgot. Your brother
          left this for you.

He fishes the envelope out of his pocket, gives it to Billy,
and starts to walk away.

Billy opens it, pulls out a wad of cash and a letter.

Billy starts to read the letter, looks up and calls after
Elliot.

                    BILLY
          Oh man. My brother -- he's
          enlisting -- the army!

                    ELLIOT
          Wow. Fuck.

                    BILLY
          You can say that again!

97A   EXT. ROUTE 17B - DAY   97A

Elliot wanders, as if in a daze, against a tide of tired,
wet, dazed concertgoers, all beginning an early exodus from
Yasgar's. Mud, trash, a vaguely excremental air -- all
matching Elliot's mood.

97B   EXT. TRAILERS - DAY   97B

We can hear intermittent feedback and the hum of an occasional announcement from the stage, as Elliot walks near the trailers by the site.

He passes by a bunch of festival volunteers who have fanned out trying to get people to move around to the side, but he pays no attention.

Just as he's about to step over/on an exposed electrical cable, Tisha shouts out to him from the steps of one of the trailers.

> TISHA
> Watch out, Elliot!

> ELLIOT
> What?

> TISHA
> The electrical wires! Come around --
> over here.

Elliot walks over to her, and touches the railing of the trailer steps, getting a small shock.

> ELLIOT
> Whoa.

> TISHA
> Yeah, everything's electric now.

From the concert site, rather than music, a loud blast of ear-piercing feedback emanates.

> TISHA (CONT'D)
> What are you up to?

> ELLIOT
> Thought I'd finally try to see the concert.

> TISHA
> Maybe later. They can't get anyone
> to play right now -- too many
> shocks. Yeah...the rain's exposed
> the lines -- the boys are in there
> trying to figure out how to switch
> 'em, or maybe they'll just give up.

                    ELLIOT
          That's a bummer. Why aren't you
          more freaked out?

                    TISHA
          Nothing us mortals can do. Either
          they pull the plug on the concert,
          and half a million hungry wet
          freaks go on a rampage across the
          Hudson Valley, or maybe they
          electrify the whole mud pool -- and
          that's a lot of grateful
          dead...like a really lot of
          grateful dead. You want a
          cigarette?

Elliot gestures no.

                    TISHA (CONT'D)
          So how's your day going?

Elliot can't quite figure out what to say.

                    ELLIOT
               (thinking)
          Well, uh....hmmm. Yeah.

                    TISHA
          The brown acid?

                    ELLIOT
          No...no...my family.

                    TISHA
          Oh. Sorry.

                    ELLIOT
          It's trivial, compared to what you
          guys are going through.

                    TISHA
          Maybe it's the most important thing
          that's happening in the whole
          universe. How do you know?

                    ELLIOT
          I'm pretty sure, it's trivial, you
          know, in perspective.

Tisha flicks her cigarette into the mud.

> TISHA
> Perspective. That's what shuts out
> the universe. Everyone has their
> own little perspective...keeps the
> love out...and I'm so tired I'm
> starting to talk like Swami
> whatshisface.

From the concert site, we hear another blast of feedback.

> ELLIOT
> Far out. But, yeah, I think you
> just made a very good point there.

She turns to go back into the trailer, getting a shock as she touches the railing.

> TISHA
> Ouch.

She and Elliot trade another smile.

> ELLIOT
> Yeah.

He watches her enter the trailer and turns to walk back.

97C   OMIT   97C

97D   INT. ELLIOT'S CABIN -- DAWN   97D

Elliot is packing up. A faint sunrise seeps through the windows.

His father knocks, enters.

> JAKE
> Hello, son.

> ELLIOT
> You're up early. Sun's barely up.

> JAKE
> I couldn't sleep.

He makes note of Elliot's packing, sits down.

                    ELLIOT
          Yeah. Hey, Dad. I was thinking. Or,
          actually, I don't know if you can
          call it thinking exactly, but I've
          been packing. I was gonna come say
          good-bye -- I hope that's ok.

                    JAKE
          Listen. Sit.

Elliot sits on the edge of the bed across from him.

                    JAKE (CONT'D)
          A week ago, I was a dying man. I
          would think to myself -- it's nice
          of Elli to come back here, to tend
          to a dying man. And who knows,
          tomorrow I could be dead. But now
          I'm alive. You understand?

                    ELLIOT
          No.

                    JAKE
          It's because of you. I'm alive
          because of you. And what should I
          want now, but for you my son to
          live too. That's not so much to
          ask.

Elliot is near tears.

                    ELLIOT
          No, it isn't.

                    JAKE
          They're all starting to leave, the
          young people. Who knows where? They
          don't even know. Now you're one of
          them. You go.

                    ELLIOT
          I'll keep in touch. I'll be back.

Jake smiles, shrugs.

                    JAKE
          Of course you will. Ah. Here, Elli,
          -- my hip.

Elliot takes his arm and helps him out of the chair.

Jake turns to him, gives him a long, tight hug.

They walk to the door.

> JAKE (CONT'D)
> (before he turns to go)
> Elli, that business with your
> mother...

> ELLIOT
> Don't worry about it.

> JAKE
> No.

> ELLIOT
> But -- I just need to know one
> thing.

> JAKE
> What?

> ELLIOT
> How have you done it? I mean, how
> have you lived with her -- more
> than forty years?

> JAKE
> (he thinks for a moment,
> smiles)
> I love her.

He lets it sink in, then turns to go.

Elliot watches his father.

98   EXT. ROAD -- DAWN   98

Elliot walks against the flow of traffic and the tired exodus
leaving the concert.

We hear the last moments of Hendrix's "Star Spangled Banner"
from afar -- the last song of the concert. Everyone on the
road has stopped to listen.

99   EXT. YASGUR'S FARM -- MORNING   99

Elliot climbs up the hill overlooking the scene, the same
spot he and the Woodstock team stood at with Max -- he's
finally arrived at the concert site.

Below him, a sea of garbage and bonfires, as 400 volunteers
collect and burn trash in the morning light.

He turns and sees Michael walking toward him. Michael leads a majestic white horse by the reins.

Michael looks over the scene with him.

> MICHAEL
> Elli, you made it.

> ELLIOT
> Yeah. Finally. It's amazing.

> MICHAEL
> It's beautiful, isn't it? Hey, and thanks for calling and welcoming us to your international resort, man. The whole world came, and now everyone's pulling together, we're gonna bring back Max's garden.

> ELLIOT
> Just like you said you would. It's all just like you said, Mike, isn't it?

> MICHAEL
> Nah, you can't say it, or even do it. You just gotta let it happen -- three days of peace and music.

> ELLIOT
> So what happens now?

> MICHAEL
> Man, who knows? Everybody's gotta chase the money now, right?...We're all probably gonna sue each other -- but that's cool. We'll figure it out. What about you?

> ELLIOT
> I don't know. I put all my stuff in my car.

> MICHAEL
> Hey, that's a sign.

Michael, with an assured elegance, mounts the horse.

                          MICHAEL (CONT'D)
          If your car moves, come look me up -
          - I'm going to San Francisco, me
          and Chip and some of the guys --
          we're gonna help out with a truly
          free concert. It's gonna be even
          more beautiful than this one.

                          ELLIOT
          Wow.

                          MICHAEL
          Yeah...The Rolling Stones.

                          ELLIOT
          The Rolling Stones?

                          MICHAEL
          Yeah, the Stones...beautiful.

And with that, Michael gently prods the horse, and rides into
the hazy field.

                          ELLIOT
                    (smiling)
          Beautiful....Beautiful!

101   Wide over the site: the cleanup, the trash, the smoke,   101
       the fires, and the mud.

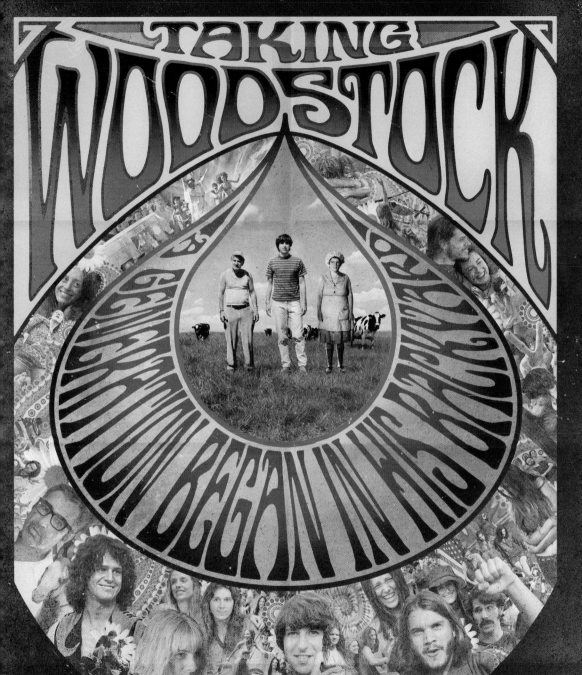

Production Notes & Stills

Remember Woodstock?

. . .Well, if you do, as the saying goes, then—you probably weren't there.

While Woodstock itself is a great subject, it's one not readily able to be captured in a film—and, furthermore, it's been done definitively; Michael Wadleigh's three-hour 1970 documentary feature *Woodstock* won an Academy Award. *Taking Woodstock* producer James Schamus, who adapted the film's script from *Taking Woodstock: A True Story of a Riot, a Concert, and a Life*, written by Elliot Tiber with Tom Monte, explains, "What we're doing is telling a tiny piece of that story, from a little corner of unexpected joy that happened almost by accident and which helped this incredible event take place."

It was almost by accident that

Opposite: Demetri Martin (left) as Elliot Tiber and Kelli Garner as VW Girl.

Above: Director Ang Lee (center) and Director of Photography Eric Gautier (left).

All photos by Ken Regan except where noted.

Tiber's tale happened to come to Schamus' longtime filmmaking partner, Academy Award-winning director/producer Ang Lee. In October 2007, Lee was booked on a San Francisco talk show to discuss their film *Lust, Caution*, which was about to open locally. Tiber was booked on the same show to discuss his book, which had recently been published. While waiting to go on, Tiber struck up a conversation with Lee, and gave Lee a copy of his memoirs.

Lee remembers, "A few days later, an old friend from film school, Pat Cupo, called. He told me he had heard Elliot had given me the book, and encouraged me to read it. "

Tiber enthuses, "Getting the 'yes' from Ang Lee was *truly* the ultimate trip. I have found in my life that whether you find the action, or the action finds you, the crucial thing is to act—and always *now*."

Lee saw *Taking Woodstock* as following naturally from his previous work. If his 1973-set movie *The Ice Storm* was, as he says, "the hangover of 1969, then *Taking Woodstock* is the beautiful night before and the last moments of innocence.

"After making several tragic movies in a row, I was looking to do a comedy—and one without cynicism. It's also a story of liberation, honesty, and tolerance—and of a 'naïve spirit' that we cannot and must not lose."

Schamus also cottoned to the project immediately, and saw bringing the film to audiences as an opportunity for "a new generation to go back and visit

Opposite, top: Concert producer Michael Lang speaking with a concertgoer at Woodstock Festival, 1969. (Photo © Henry Diltz/Corbis).

Bottom: (front row, left to right) Mamie Gummer as Tisha, Jonathan Groff as Michael Lang, Kevin Sussman as Stan, and Demetri Martin as Elliot Tiber.

Above: Demetri Martin and screenwriter James Schamus.

Woodstock and get a feel for what it must've been like when you could have hope, and really move some mountains and enjoy it.

"Because we embraced that ethos, Ang actually enjoyed the hard work on this film. This is Ang's and my eleventh film together; he keeps raising the stakes for himself and meeting new challenges."

To make *Taking Woodstock*, the pair was joined by two-time Emmy Award-winning producer Celia Costas. She notes, "Ang Lee was going to be making a movie about when I came of age, almost in my backyard—an opportunity I couldn't pass up!

"In the late 1960s, the world was your oyster, whether politically or socially. We were in the middle of a war, but despite that it was such a positive time and we felt that if we got together we could do anything. That's something which has sorely been missed, and perhaps we are trying to begin to recapture that now."

Costas found that "with his script, James created a smart and funny world that Ang can flourish in; he's able to give Ang situations and concepts that Ang, as a unique humanist filmmaker, can—and does—run with."

Schamus notes, "Underneath all the comedy in this movie are emotions, and meditations on what it means for people to transform themselves."

In those respects, this latest work harkens back to the Lee/Schamus team's earliest collaborations, while also continuing Lee's career-long exploration of familial/generational dynamics. For Elliot and his Jewish immigrant parents Sonia and Jake Teichberg (portrayed in the film by

Opposite: Demetri Martin as Elliot Tiber and Eugene Levy as Max Yasgur.

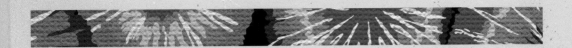

acclaimed U.K. actors Imelda Staunton and Henry Goodman), getting unexpectedly caught up in the preparations for Woodstock gifts them all with a learning experience, and then some; "For the first time in their lives, they have the opportunity to emotionally reveal themselves to one another," notes Costas.

Schamus adds, "In the midst of a great cultural moment, Elliot comes to fully accept who he is. His gay identity is part of the story, and so is his identity as his own man—not just as his parents' son. Woodstock is freeing and transforming for all three of them, but it's Elliot's life that's the most positively impacted."

CASTING

Demetri Martin, of the hit cable series *Important Things with Demetri Martin*, makes his feature starring debut as Elliot Tiber in *Taking Woodstock*. His and Jonathan Groff's casting are just the latest examples of Lee's eliciting breakout performances from fresh talent in his movies; Martin had been brought to the attention of the filmmakers by Schamus' teenaged daughter, who had urged her father to watch a clip of one of Martin's comedy routines ("The Jokes with Guitar") on YouTube.

Viewing additional routines and footage, Schamus had liked what he saw, which was a presence conveying "a ferocity of intelligence, coupled with a non-assaultive style and vulnerability that is unusual in a stand-up comic."

Just as the story had suddenly found Lee, Martin's audition and screen tests convinced the director and Schamus that they had found their leading man. "I'd never worked with a comedian," muses Lee. "But we made a very good choice. You want to see more of Demetri; you like him, he's a fresh face.

Opposite, top: Demetri Martin as Elliot Tiber at Yasgur's farm.

Bottom: Demetri Martin as Elliot Tiber and Jonathan Groff as Michael Lang.

"In his demeanor and his disposition, he is very close to the characterization in the script. Plus, he's genuinely funny."

Martin says, "In stand-up I'm trying to be myself. Doing this meant I would have to be someone else, and interpret another writer's words and storyline."

The actor was immediately intrigued by the emotional arc of his role. He notes, "When we first meet Elliot, he doesn't have a real relationship with anybody. He seems kind of stuck between obligation to his family and cutting the cord. Guilt seems to be a big part of what keeps him in the kind of behavioral patterns he's in.

"For me, this was an exciting opportunity to work with Ang Lee and learn about acting." Martin did just that, logging three weeks of rehearsal prior to the start of filming and also spending time with Tiber "to ask him about some specific details."

Costas assesses Martin as having "great timing and great instincts. He's perfect for Elliot, like Dustin Hoffman was perfect for *The Graduate*."

By the spring of 2008, the project was quickly coalescing. As always, Lee went to great lengths to marshal research. David Silver, hired as the film's historian, was given a mandate to put together what became known as the "Hippie Handbook," a compendium of articles, timelines, essays, and a glossary of "Hippie Lingo," from "freak out" to "roach clip." Even words that had long permeated the culture were re-investigated. Silver reveals, "The first hippies were 19th-century German immigrants who came to Northern California and lived a communal agrarian lifestyle. Some decades later, the term 'hippie' derived from 'hipster' and 'hip,' the idea being that these people as a whole were cool. The word has a light feeling, and did not necessarily mean someone was radical, or an activist. They were more interested in smaller, interactive changes between and among people."

Lee clarifies another point, noting that "Woodstock didn't happen *in* Woodstock. But we don't think of it as 'White Lake' or 'Bethel,' we say 'Woodstock.'"

Opposite: Jonathan Groff as Michael Lang.

Location filming was set for New York State's Columbia and Rensselaer Counties, as well as a couple of days in New York City. *Taking Woodstock* was one of the first films to take advantage of the enhanced (by 300%) incentives and tax credits that the state now offers; the production boosted the local economy with millions of dollars.

So it was that *Taking Woodstock* moved rapidly towards production—on a parallel summertime track to the three-day Woodstock Music and Arts Festival of peace and music's own trajectory 39 years prior. For full convergence, the film released in theaters on the 40th Anniversary weekend of Woodstock.

Below: (left to right) Henry Goodman as Jake, Demetri Martin as Elliot, and Imelda Staunton as Sonia.

Opposite, top: Director Ang Lee. Bottom: The camera crew shooting the crowds arriving for the festival.

I n 1969, the dream-into-action was being realized by Wood-stock Ventures' Michael Lang (played in *Taking Woodstock* by Groff), Artie Kornfeld (played by Adam Pally), Joel Rosenman (Daniel Eric Gold), and John Roberts (Skylar Astin). Lang had emerged as a memorable figure in the documentary *Woodstock*, and no less so in Tiber's account of his own encounters with him. From one producer to another, Schamus praises Lang—who visited the set, met with the filmmakers, and spent time with Groff—as someone "who sometimes put being a businessman first, as he had to—yet he never seemed cynical. It must have been incredibly exhausting; he had to maintain this aura of a beautiful hippie.

"Jonathan—whose first movie this is—precisely caught the wave of all of those nuances in Michael's character."

Lee worked with Groff to get a performance from the actor capturing, as Groff puts it, "the vibe of Michael—which I had experienced firsthand—while also freeing it up and finding my own version," while Groff continued to watch the documentary's scenes showing Lang over and over again each day on the set before filming began.

Beyond sporting the fringed leather vest and long brown curls, the actor aimed for capturing the way Lang stood for "the magical quality of Woodstock while also dealing with the nuts and bolts of putting together a concert and hiring a staff and getting everything done," representing Woodstock in more ways than one.

"They really launched it on a wing and a prayer," marvels Costas. "That weekend, there was rain and heat and confusion and traffic and hunger—every element you can possibly think of, except maybe a plague of locusts. But a legacy was beautifully defined in a single weekend.

"So, while the organization of the festival is integral to the comedy at our film's heart, the festival is still very

Opposite, top left: The real Elliot Tiber, 1969. (Courtesy of Elliot Tiber)

Top right: The real Max Yasgur on his farm, 1970. (© AP Photo)

Bottom: Demetri Martin as Elliot Tiber and Eugene Levy as Max Yasgur.

much a backdrop to our central story of Elliot and his family and friends' epiphanies."

The uphill quest undertaken by Lang and his team of festival organizers complements the underdog story of Elliot and his transformation over the course of the summer of 1969. Yet, as executive producer Michael Hausman notes, "literally and figuratively, the festival remains just over the hill from the motel and the people there."

As Schamus points out, "If anyone is coming into the movie waiting to see who plays and lip-synchs Janis Joplin at the festival, well, that's not in *Taking Woodstock* and was never going to be."

Instead, a transformative human story is placed in the context of a transformative cultural event.

As comedy icon Eugene Levy reflects, "The timing was right for Woodstock; it was at the end of probably the most dynamic decade of the 20th century. I have to admit I didn't know a lot about Woodstock before it happened, but on the weekend it was underway, it started hitting the news in a major way."

Martin marvels, "I've been a fan of Eugene's since I was a kid. The role of Max is one different than people are used to seeing him do, and in my scenes with him I felt like I was lucky to have a front-row seat."

"Ang wanted me to look and sound like Max as much as I could," reveals Levy. "I read up on Max and looked at what little footage exists. Ang described Max to me as an old-school Republican—the Abe Lincoln kind, who respected the freedoms that the party stood for initially.

"Woodstock was a business venture for him, and Max grew to love what it turned into. He had suffered a serious health crisis about a year before, and after that he decided that nothing seemed quite so scary or intimidating. He stood among the townspeople and said, 'There's nothing wrong with these kids.'"

In counterpoint, Jeffrey Dean Morgan is cast as Dan, whom

the actor describes as "a community leader, seemingly happily married but not. The town he's part of is set in its ways, and the residents are none too happy that thousands of hippies are coming to town. But the world, and their world, is about to change. Who would have thought that a concert could do that."

Even a concert whose attendance organically grew and grew and grew, benefitting the town and its people. Levy acknowledges, "Yes, Max bumped his price up when he heard how many people were coming, but he told the promoters that he would back them up—and he did. So, he was a man of his word *and* a good businessman."

The "good businessman" description could not be applied to the Teichbergs, but, as Levy notes, "Elliot and his parents made a lot of money in a short time. It's a turning point for them."

Goodman, as the Teichberg patriarch, sees the family's benefits as more than financial. He emphasizes, "Each person, in their different way, moves forward in positive steps

Above: Jonathan Groff as Michael Lang and Demetri Martin as Elliot Tiber.

through the course of the movie."

Martin remarks, "At first, the family's lives are joyless; Jake and Sonia feel kind of stuck with each other."

While Goodman had known Staunton from having starred together onstage years prior, he was gratified at how "Ang worked to start a dialogue among our on-screen family. He was keen for Imelda and Demetri and me to come together for over a week. That way, by the time of filming, we could connect to each other and get to places very quickly as actors."

Costas lauds the actor's ability to convey "how Jake, who is so unhappy, comes alive and opens up like a flower. Henry is wonderful in the role."

Schamus states, "By the end of the movie, he and his son have made a real connection—and it's not at the expense of Mom."

With her nature forged by her immigrant history, Elliot's perpetually disapproving mother Sonia is the source of comedic moments in the film. But, as Staunton notes, "Those come from a very dark place—which, of course, most of the best comedy comes from. Ang and I discussed how I would not be playing it for laughs. What Sonia grew up with in Russia has never left her.

"Therapy-speak doesn't exist in her and Jake's lives. They haven't got a large emotional vocabulary. There's nothing better for an actor than to get hold of a good character; I do what's right for the part."

Opposite, top: Imelda Staunton as Sonia.

Bottom: Henry Goodman as Jake.

Above: (left to right) Henry Goodman as Jake, Imelda Staunton as Sonia, and Demetri Martin as Elliot.

Staunton's modesty belies her commitment to fleshing out the character; as costume designer Joseph G. Aulisi remembers, "I spoke to Imelda on the

phone from London. She said, 'You've got to give me some help because I move much too quickly,' and we all saw Sonia as a more rotund woman. So I designed a body pad, which we filled with birdseed and adapted to some actual early 1960s housedresses so that it would move with her body. It worked well enough that most people didn't recognize her without her body pad and her wig.

"Now, most actresses will not wear something sleeveless, but Imelda wanted the housedresses that way. She gets so into the part that everything she does is made believable, with her wonderful physicality."

In contrast to the petite Staunton stands 6'3" actor Liev Schreiber as Vilma, the cross-dressing ex-Marine who joins the Woodstock preparations by becoming security detail at the El Monaco hotel. Vilma's mere presence helps cue an essential realization for Elliot that he must live his life as a

gay man "and he ever so gently encourages Jake and Sonia to live their lives, too," notes Costas.

Lee sees Schreiber's character as "someone who has found peace within himself, though not without struggle, and is therefore a role model for Elliot.

"We are all very complicated creatures. How can all these elements—wartime experience, cross-dressing, goodness—coexist in one person? But they do, and it's not Vilma's problem; if it's anyone's, it's yours. This was a true acting test for Liev."

Schamus adds, "As played by Liev, Vilma is a force of nature. Like all of the other characters, she has her own transformations that happen."

Schreiber, in his research, "found that the whole gender-bending movement was very active by 1969. Vilma embodies contradictions, not only of sexuality but also in her own character. Those contradictions were the most interesting part of the role for me. She hasn't stopped being masculine, and hasn't stopped being feminine; she just is, she doesn't worry about judgment, and she is generous and protective.

"Since I'd done it before, I had no real concerns over playing a man in a dress. Well, there is always the concern that you might not look good in a dress."

Aulisi remarks, "We capitalized on Liev's height and biceps, and made it work for us. Headbands helped give Vilma a female aura. Ang and I had initially sparked to a scrapbook I found which showed men who went to the Catskills in the late 1950s and dressed up as women. Then, with Liev's input, we updated Vilma's wardrobe to the late 1960s and made it more casual and comfortable—reflecting the freedom that was starting to happen."

More freely expressive from the get-go are the local avant-garde theater troupe the Earthlight Players. Aulisi laughs, "I got a lot of horrible yellows together for them, and since they have no money we did very easy costumes that could have been made by them—and could come off easily!"

Dan Fogler, cast as Earthlight Players leader Devon, calls the group "very serious actors who do very silly things with their bodies." To make sure that the actor would be a credible troupe head, Lee encouraged Fogler to work closely with choreographer Joann Jensen on coordinating the group's surprising turns.

Fogler remarks, "I was told how particular Ang is, and he's an incredible captain of the ship, but he also brought a sense of trust and a sense of play—he would get up there and do the troupe's moves to show us what he wanted!"

Production designer David Gropman notes, "The wonderful thing about Ang is

Opposite, top: Liev Schreiber (left) as Vilma and Demetri Martin as Elliot.

Bottom: Henry Goodman (left) as Jake and Liev Schreiber as Vilma.

Above: The Earthlight Players.

149

how he undertook to completely understand the world and the culture and the time that the story took place in."

Lee remarks, "Working on *Taking Woodstock*, I began to feel a passion for the '60s."

But even this pales in comparison to the director/producer's passion for detail. Weeks before filming began, Lee gave Groff—who was then in the midst of performing in a revival of *Hair*—a binder of assembled research as well as 10 mix CDs of important music from the late 1960s *and* DVDs of some 20 movies from and about the period.

Emile Hirsch, cast as Vietnam vet Billy, offers, "That attention to detail is what makes Ang's films so rich. Ang sent me probably *30* DVDs; *Apocalypse Now*, *The Deer Hunter*, *Platoon*, *Full Metal Jacket*, *Hamburger Hill*, the documentary *Winter Soldier*...not just Vietnam-themed films but World War II movies as well—and *Fantastic Voyage*, which was amazing!

"Another key assignment that Ang had me do was to go to a shooting range to get some experience. I also met with an Iraq War veteran who took me through his own experience and discussed post-traumatic stress disorder (PTSD) with me, since that is something that Billy has."

Passion for the Details

Veteran costume designer Aulisi marvels, "I have never worked with a director who has done so much homework, and who has such an incredible vision of what he wants to achieve. He remembers every photograph you have ever shown him. He knew the material so well and cared about it so much that it was impossible for us not to care as much and share his vision.

"Overall, we used as many genuine clothes from the period as we could get, gathering an enormous amount of clothing from over 50 different sources. But on days calling for many extras [a.k.a.

background artists], clothes had to be physically executed in a couple of hours. 1969 marked a major turning point in fashion—although the townspeople are slightly behind the times, so their look is more early 1960s/Montgomery Ward catalogue."

Lee and his team assembled a "war room," where a massive flow chart/spreadsheet was posted on a 30-foot wall. Post-Its in every imaginable hue chronologically marked both the shooting days and the days of the action in the film, and emotional and physical progress of characters as well as the usual issues of continuity; e.g., what color the water in the motel pool should be from scene to scene. Also marked were what Lee and historian Silver called "vignettes;" little scraps of information and kernels of interest gleaned from Tiber's book, the documentary feature and other filmed and photographic records, and all the assembled research.

Costas reports, "We were steeped in what people were listening to and reading; what art they were looking at;

Above: Emile Hirsch as Billy.

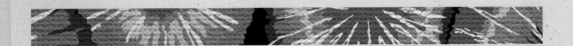

and what programs *and* commercials they were watching on television. It was multimedia exposure. Certainly, there was a lot about the festival that we weren't aware of."

One cluster of information posted, for instance, centered around food: how, during the festival, it nearly ran out (the few commercial concessions sold out early, and the town's coffers were nearly depleted) until everyone benefited from the efforts of the Hog Farm, the hippie group from California (founded about two years earlier by Hugh Romney, a.k.a. Wavy Gravy) who cooked and dished out food for free.

Another "vignette" was a scene inspired by the documentary, of a man painting a daisy on a woman's face; Lee wanted it—and many more—re-created in the film, as part of cinematographer Eric Gautier's capturing the essence of the period and the Woodstock ethos.

Lee reminds that "in all this source material, there can be differing versions of what happened. Eventually, you have to decide at what times to take creative license."

Indeed, what came up in the "war room" ran contrary to 40 years' worth of shared perceptions. Schamus reveals, "The people who went to Woodstock were not all hippies with long hair and sideburns smoking joints. Although those are the pictures that ended up being reproduced the most, a lot of the attendees didn't look that different than young people do today. Our decision was, let's access the 'expected' look, but also give the reality."

To further quantify; the team's research had determined that hippies—who tended to be nomadic in nature, traveling from event to event—had arrived at the festival site first, followed by college kids—some, but by no means all, with longish hair—and then by the other 85% of the attendees, high school students and other assorted

Opposite, top: Jefferson Airplane on stage playing before the massive audience at Woodstock, 1969. (Photo © Henry Diltz/ Corbis)

Bottom: Audience leaving Woodstock Festival, 1969. (Photo © Henry Diltz/Corbis)

"straights"—people who had shorter hair and generally wore nondescript clothing.

Accordingly, the flow chart on the wall was amended by Lee to divide up the background artists into seven "tribes"; among them the Willow Tribe, the Biker Tribe, and the Pool Tribe. Script supervisor Mary Cybulski reports, "This was so that when we actually got on the set and there were hundreds of extras, culled from our open casting calls across five states, we knew who should be doing what and when—and where they fit in."

Lee points out, "This was also so I could *see* them better—there were hundreds of people!"

Extras casting director Sophia Costas reveals, "We were so fortunate to find a lot of people who live communally today, and who are committed to living by the tenets that the young people at Woodstock were trying to espouse. Some of these people 'looked right' because they really lived—and live—that life, and were able to present themselves purely and innocently, which shows up on camera.

"Ang took an interest in the extras casting, and wanted to make sure we showed how this event was a meeting place for *all* different types of philosophies and people, who co-existed peacefully for three days. So you will see everyone from Hare Krishnas to Hasidic Jews on-screen."

Schamus points out that "there was not one single reported incident of violence at Woodstock. There was just celebration."

Cybulski adds, "Ang wanted to make sure that we really felt the rush, the flood of all these people and new ideas coming through a small town. So he wanted the background artists to be very specific. Lots of times in movies they're just people hanging out, but he wanted something more potent."

Opposite, top: Kelli Garner as VW Girl and Paul Dano as VW Guy.

Bottom: The camera crew shooting the mud sliding scene.

Second second assistant director Tudor Jones elaborates, "Ang's scrutiny

is all-encompassing. Even if someone is 300 yards from the lens, he will want that person to be in the right posture with the right attitude and the right look—and he's very sensitive to someone who's not at the right emotional level in the scene, so he'll keep doing it until he finds it to be right.

"You feel like your job is worth it, unlike with directors who don't notice the hard work you're putting in."

Lee also sought the ideal barn for the scenes with the Earthlight Players. The search yielded one—in New Hampshire. So Lee had the structure disassembled piece by piece and trucked to the location shoot—where it was then put back together. Once shooting wrapped, the barn was returned.

An even bigger logistical challenge facing the production was staging the so-called S-road scene, in which a state trooper carries Elliot on the back of his motorcycle from the motel towards the concert site. The motorcycle weaves through an enormous line of stalled traffic—and festivalgoers on foot—backed up along a serpentine road almost as far as the eye can see. Calling for hundreds of extras and over 100 vehicles, the scene was successfully filmed in just one day.

"With our great crew, we got it—and without one complaint, from either background artists or townspeople! It was *the* most challenging scene," asserts Hausman. "Here, too, we had iconic images we wanted to reproduce. With a re-creation of this magnitude, we did rehearse it the day before."

The majority of the 42-day shoot ended up taking place in the town of New Lebanon, in Columbia County—marking the first time that a major motion picture had been filmed there.

Residents' vintage cars—from "Love Bug" Volkswagens to panel vans—were back in their element for scenes, some for their last mile; picture car coordinator Philip Schneider reports, "Several of these were just hanging on, and during the S-road scene, a number fell by the wayside."

A retired but still intact motel, the Valley Rest, was put back into temporary operation and re-dressed and restructured by Gropman and his crew to play the (no longer existing) El Monaco. "True to the actual motel and all of those Catskills motels of that era, everything was painted white," points out Gropman. "We did put little splashes of color on some of the trim and doorways—working from photographic records and re-creating what Elliot had done."

Schamus praises Gropman "and his whole team for studying Elliot's family history, and the history of the Catskills and what it meant to be a Jewish family out there. When you walked onto that location, you were seeing these lives as they were lived."

The Hitchinpost Café met one of the production's most specific requests by delivering 500 eaten corn cobs for a scene, after making sure that local schoolchildren were given the corn first as a free lunch.

Above: (left to right) Elliot Tiber, Demetri Martin, and Ang Lee.

"Without the enhanced tax credit incentive, we never could have filmed in New York State," asserts Celia Costas.

157

"Rarely have any of us had a better location filming experience. The people from the town of New Lebanon, and throughout Columbia and Rensselaer Counties, were warm and welcoming and became terrific partners in the experience of making the film."

Throughout the production, environmental steward Nicole Feder oversaw implementation of an extensive on-set recycling program. For the scenes requiring hundreds of extras, water stations and/or stainless steel water canteens staved off use of plastic water bottles and accompanying waste. It was all, as Celia Costas notes, "in keeping with the spirit of the movie."

Comparing environmental efforts across the decades, Schamus point out that "while there were 600 acres of trash left behind at Woodstock, 400 volunteers did stay and clean it up. So even *that* was beautiful!

"Woodstock was three days of peace and music, and this was three months of peace and movie."

Lee concludes, "With our great cast and crew, we felt the energy and the spirit of the Woodstock experience. We had a blast!" ✌

Below: Behind-the-scenes shot of the crowd of revelers growing larger before the start of the festival.

TIMELINE:
THE ROAD TO WOODSTOCK

1935 Eliyahu Teichberg (whose name is later changed to Elliot Tiber) is born in Brooklyn, New York, to Jewish immigrant parents

1955 Jacob (Jake) and Sonia Teichberg, the parents of Elliot Tiber, buy the El Monaco Motel in White Lake, New York, and operate it with their son

December 1960 The birth of "The Pill," a birth-control method that effectively revolutionizes sex

1963 Betty Friedan's *The Feminine Mystique* is published, marking the beginning of modern feminism

August 28, 1963 During the Civil Rights March on Washington, Dr. Martin Luther King, Jr., delivers his "I Have a Dream" speech

Nov. 22, 1963 President John F. Kennedy is assassinated; Lyndon B. Johnson is sworn in as President

February 9 and 16, 1964 The Beatles appear on *The Ed Sullivan Show*

July 2, 1964 The Civil Rights Act is passed

August 2, 1964 The Gulf of Tonkin incident in Southeast Asia, where the Viet Cong are waging war in South Vietnam and the U.S. has been building up troops, spurs the Senate to pass the Gulf of Tonkin Resolution urging LBJ to wage war against Vietnam without a Declaration of War

February 21, 1965 Nation of Islam leader Malcolm X is assassinated

March 21, 1965 First anti-Vietnam War Teach-In is held

January 14, 1967 "Human Be-In" is held in San Francisco's Golden Gate Park, drawing about 30,000; Timothy Leary coins directive "Turn on, tune in, drop out"

June 16-18, 1967 The Monterey International Pop Festival, held at the Monterey County Fairgrounds in California, showcases many performers who would also play at Woodstock two years later; about 200,000 people attend; the documentary feature *Monterey Pop* is released the following year

Summer 1967 The Summer of Love unfolds in San Francisco, becoming a flashpoint for the full flowering of the hippie movement as thousands of high school- and college-age students head to the city

March 16, 1968 My Lai massacre in Vietnam

April 4, 1968 Dr. Martin Luther King, Jr., is assassinated

June 6, 1968 Robert F. Kennedy is assassinated

January 20, 1969 The inauguration of Richard M. Nixon as President

February 20, 1969 President Nixon approves the bombing of Cambodia

March 11, 1969 Levi's begins to sell bell-bottomed blue jeans

March 19, 1969 The Chicago 7 are indicted in the aftermath of the previous summer's violent Chicago Democratic Convention protests

May 15, 1969 University of California officials fence People's Park in Berkeley despite protests of 3000 people to save it; Governor Ronald Reagan places Berkeley under martial law; one protester is shot and killed

May 23, 1969 The Who release their rock-opera album *Tommy*

June 22, 1969 Judy Garland dies

June 27-28, 1969 The Stonewall Riots (so named for the Stonewall Inn bar, which was targeted for police harassment) erupt in New York City, marking the beginning of the Gay Liberation movement; Elliot Tiber is among the active participants in the Riots

July 14, 1969 Michael Lang and his fellow producers Joel Rosenman and John Roberts are denied a permit for a music and arts festival in Wallkill, New York

July 15, 1969 Hearing that the festival's permit has been denied, Elliot Tiber contacts Michael Lang

July 18, 1969 In an accident, Senator Ted Kennedy's car plunges off the Chappaquiddick Bridge, and his passenger Mary Jo Kopechne dies

July 18, 1969 Festival-goers begin to arrive and camp out at the festival site

July 20, 1969 The U.S. lands the first man on the moon

August 9, 1969 Members of Charles Manson's "Family" slay pregnant actress Sharon Tate and four others in California

August 15–18, 1969 "Woodstock Music & Art Fair presents An Aquarian Exposition in Bethel, N.Y.; 3 Days of Peace & Music;" approximately half a million people attend, and more try and fail to get to the site; performers include Joan Baez, Joe Cocker, Country Joe and the Fish, Richie Havens, Jimi Hendrix, Jefferson Airplane, Janis Joplin, The Who, and two dozen more acts

September 26, 1969 The Beatles' album *Abbey Road* is released

November 15, 1969 250,000 people peacefully demonstrate against the Vietnam War in Washington, D.C.

December 6, 1969 The Rolling Stones concert at Altamont Speedway in California, where Hell's Angels were hired as security, sees violent fighting break out and four people die; footage from the concert is seen the following year in the documentary feature *Gimme Shelter*

March 1970 Michael Wadleigh's three-hour documentary *Woodstock* is released, as is the film's soundtrack

April 10, 1971 *Woodstock* does not win the Academy Awards for Best Film Editing and Best Sound, but the picture does win the Academy Award for Best Documentary Feature

GLOSSARY

Back in 1969, the following words held meanings beyond their dictionary ones…

Axe: Any musical instrument, or any tool you use to do your art

Ball: (as a noun) A good time; (as a verb) Sexual intercourse

Bread: Money ("I'm broke—man, can you lay some bread on me?")

Freak: Insiders' synonym for hippie (possibly coined by Frank Zappa)

Fuzz: The police

Gas: Sublime ("They've never sounded better—that was a gas!")

Head: Insiders' term for a member of the counterculture (possibly coined by Ken Kesey)

Lid: An ounce of marijuana

Mike: Microgram

Pig: Hippies' term for the police

Rap: To speak/communicate in the language of hip

Ripped: Under the influence of an illegal substance

Roach: A small butt of marijuana

CAST AND CREW CREDITS

FOCUS FEATURES
presents
an ANG LEE film

"TAKING WOODSTOCK"

DEMETRI MARTIN   DAN FOGLER   HENRY GOODMAN   JONATHAN GROFF   EUGENE LEVY
JEFFREY DEAN MORGAN   IMELDA STAUNTON   with EMILE HIRSCH and LIEV SCHREIBER
SKYLAR ASTIN   KEVIN CHAMBERLIN   KELLI GARNER   DANIEL ERIC GOLD
MAMIE GUMMER   EDWARD HIBBERT   STEPHEN KUNKEN   JENNIFER MERRILL
ADAM PALLY   KEVIN SUSSMAN   RICHARD THOMAS

casting by AVY KAUFMAN, C.S.A.	production designer DAVID GROPMAN	produced by JAMES SCHAMUS ANG LEE CELIA COSTAS
costume Designer JOSEPH G. AULISI	director of photography ERIC GAUTIER, AFC	
music by DANNY ELFMAN	executive producer MICHAEL HAUSMAN	screenplay by JAMES SCHAMUS
associate producer DAVID LEE	based on the book by ELLIOT TIBER with TOM MONTE	directed by ANG LEE
editor TIM SQUYRES, A.C.E.		

CAST
(In order of appearance)

Jake Teichberg . . . . . . HENRY GOODMAN
British Gentleman. . . . . EDWARD HIBBERT
Sonia Teichberg . . . . . IMELDA STAUNTON
Elliot Teichberg . . . . . . DEMETRI MARTIN
Jackson Spiers . . . . . KEVIN CHAMBERLIN
George the Doorman . . . TAKEO LEE WONG
Esther. . . . . ANTHOULA KATSIMATIDES
Frank . . . . CLARK MIDDLETON
Annie. . . . . BETTE HENRITZE
Margaret. . . . . SONDRA JAMES
Dan . . . . JEFFREY DEAN MORGAN
Carol . . . . CHRISTINA KIRK
Town Clerk . . . . GAIL MARTINO
Billy . . . . EMILE HIRSCH
Dave. . . . . ADAM LEFEVRE
Max Yasgur . . . . EUGENE LEVY
Bob. . . . . ANDY PROSKY
Devon . . . . DAN FOGLER
Earthlight Players . . . . CARMEL AMIT
ZACHARY BOOTH
JENNIFER MERRILL
IVAN SANDOMIRE

Earthlight Players (cont.) . . MATTHEW SHEAR
DARCY BLEDSOE
HALLEY CIANFARINI
JESSE KILE
ASHLEY MIDDLEBROOK
BEC STUPACK
Steven . . . . GABRIEL SUNDAY
Michael Lang . . . . JONATHAN GROFF
Tisha . . . . MAMIE GUMMER
Mel . . . . STEPHEN KUNKEN
Artie Kornfeld. . . . . ADAM PALLY
Stan . . . . KEVIN SUSSMAN
Miriam. . . . . PIPPA PEARTHREE
John Roberts . . . . SKYLAR ASTIN
Joel Rosenman. . . . . . DANIEL ERIC GOLD
Angry Diner Patrons . . LEONARD BERDICK
SHARON J. GIROUX
WILLIAM B. WARD, JR.
Hippie Girl. . . . . LOUISA KRAUSE
Hippie Guy . . . . . . SPADAQUE VOLCIMUS
Inspectors . . . . BILL COELIUS
NICK TAYLOR
John Morris. . . . . . MICHAEL IZQUIERDO
Penny. . . . . . . KATHERINE WATERSTON

Chip Monck . . . . WILL JANOWITZ
Steve Cohen. . . . . JEREMY SHAMOS
Wes Pomeroy . . . . . . MALACHY CLEARY
Reverend Don . . . . . RICHARD THOMAS
Assistants . . . . SEBASTIAN BEACON
KELLY KLEIN
Woodstock Ventures PA . . . GARRETT ROSS
Paul . . . . DARREN PETTIE
Hippie in Line. . . . . ANDREW KATZ
Charlie. . . . . PATRICK CUPO
Doug . . . . BORIS McGIVER
Vilma . . . . LIEV SCHREIBER
Young Woman . . . . CAITLIN FITZGERALD
Journalists. . . . . MICHAEL J. BURG
TAUNIA HOTTMAN-HUBBARD
DAVID LAVINE
Young Man #1 . . . . MICHAEL ZEGEN
Sam . . . . ANDREW ZOX
Hairy Pretzel . . . . ANGUS HAMILTON
CHRISTOPHER MEIER
RICHARD PHELAN McGREAL
CASSON RUGEN
JOSEPH ULMER
Young Guy at Phone . . . . . HARRY ZITTEL
Young Girl at Phone . . . ALYSSA MAY GOLD
Bongo Player. . . . GASTON JEAN-BAPTISTE
Flutist . . . . MICHAEL McGINNIS
Guitar Player. . . . . DAN KNOBLER
Congo Player . . . . JON SEALE
News Reporter. . . DAVID WILSON BARNES
State Trooper . . . . JAMES HANLON
Young Man #2. . STEFANO STEVEN DA FRE
Dealer . . . . DON PUGLISI
Bra Burners . . . . KIRSTEN BACH
RACHEL MORRALL
VW Guy . . . . PAUL DANO
VW Girl . . . . KELLI GARNER
St. Paul Lady. . . . MARGORIE AUSTRIAN
Interviewer . . . . KYLE PLANTE
Worker. . . . . LEW ZUCKER
Stunt Coordinator . . . . . . BRIAN K. SMYJ
Stunts . . . . EUGENE HARRISON
ANDY ARMSTRONG
NORMAN DOUGLASS
KIMBERLY SHANNON MURPHY
MICK O'ROURKE
Pilots . . . . WILLIAM RICHARDS
GEORGE MICHAEL PEAVEY
WILLIAM G. WRIGHT

Produced in Association with
Twins Financing LLC
Unit Production Manager . . . CELIA COSTAS

First Assistant Director
. . . . MICHAEL HAUSMAN

Second Assistant Director . . PETER THORELL
Associate Producers . . . . . PATRICK CUPO
DAVID SAUERS
Production Supervisor . . . . DEB DYER
Post Production Supervisor . . JENNIFER LANE
Historical Consultant . . . . . DAVID SILVER
Art Director . . . . PETER ROGNESS
Assistant Art Directors . . . . . ADAM SCHER
MICHAEL AUSZURA
JOHN POLLARD
Set Decorator
. . . . . ELLEN CHRISTIANSEN DE JONGE
A-Camera Operator . . . . . . ERIC GAUTIER
First Assistant A-Camera. . CHRIS REYNOLDS
Second Assistant A-Camera. . ETHAN BORSUK
B-Camera Operator/Steadicam Operator
. . . . CARLOS GUERRA
VFX Director of Photography
. . . . PATRICK CAPONE
First Assistant B-Camera
. . . . STANLEY FERNANDEZ
Second Assistant B-Camera
. . . . JULIAN DELACRUZ
Loader. . . . . MARITZA NORR
Additional Operator . . . . . JON DELGADO
First Assistant C-Camera
. . . . CHRISTOPHER RAYMOND
Second Assistants C-Camera
. . . . LISA ORIGLIERI
MATT BALZARINI
Camera / VFX Production Assistant
. . . . ALEX LIPSCHULTZ
Camera Production Assistant . . COLIN FELTH
Still Photographer
. . . . KEN REGAN / CAMERA 5
Script Supervisor . . . . . MARY CYBULSKI
Production Sound Mixer . . . . DREW KUNIN
Boom Operators . . . MARK GOODERMOTE
KIRA SMITH
First Assistant Editor. . . . . MIKE FAY
Apprentice Editor . . . . . FRED NORTHRUP
Post Production Coordinator
. . . . LESLIE BAUTSCH
Post Production Assistants
. . . . CATHERINE SHAO
GARDNER GOULD
Assistant Costume Designer
. . . . REBECCA HOFHERR
Additional Assistant Costume Designers
. . . MEREDITH MARKWORTH-POLLACK
AUTUMN SAVILLE

Costume Supervisors . . . . J. KEVIN DRAVES
DAVID DAVENPORT
Set Costumers. . . . . . . VALENTINA AULISI
NICOLE GREENBAUM
Costumers. . . . . TINA ULEE
GERALD CRAWFORD
DENISE ANDRES
MICHELLE TEAGUE
JOSEPH LA CORTE
LAUREN SCHAD
CHERYL KILBOURNE-KIMPTON
NINA CINELLI
CHUCK CRUTCHFIELD
LAURA DOWNING
Makeup Department Head . . . LUANN CLAPS
Key Makeup Artist . . . . . NICKY PATTISON
Make Up Artist . . . . . JOSEPH CAMPAYNO
Additional Make Up Artists
. . . . CARL FULLERTON
SUNDAY ENGLIS
Hair Department Head . . LYNDELL QUIYOU
Key Hair. . . . . JERRY DeCARLO
Hair . . . . CHERYL DANIELS
Additional Hair. . . . . PEGGY SCHIERHOLZ
Chief Lighting Technician . . . GENE ENGELS
Best Boy Electric . . . . JIM GREGORY
Rigging Gaffer . . . . . FRANCIS J. McBRIDE
Rigging Best Boy Electric
. . . . LOUIS PETRAGLIA
Lamp Operators . . . . LEWIS SADLER
STEVE McNALLY
SEAN McCARDELL
DAVID ELWELL
Rigging Electrics. . . . . . . STEVEN EDICK
GLENN DAVIS
Basecamp . . . . KYLE STEPHENS
Genny Operator . . . . PHILIP TESTA
Key Grip. . . . . GEORGE PATSOS
Best Boy Grip . . . . GUS MAGALIOS
Dolly Grip . . . . LOUIS SABAT
Key Rigging Grip . . . . . . WILLIAM PATSOS
Best Boy Rigging Grip . . . . . . SONNY REA
Grips. . . . . KEVIN GILLIGAN
MICHAEL URICH
RONALD WATERS
KEVIN CALIFANO
RALPH REA
Rigging Grip . . . . ROCCO PROSCIA
Property Master . . . . . . SANDY HAMILTON
Props . . . . JOEL WEAVER
RYAN WEBB
Special Effects Coordinator
. . . . STEVE KIRSHOFF
On Set Special Effects . . JOHN R. STIFANICH

Special Effects . . . . JOSEPH MARTIN
DEVIN MAGGIO
JACK KIRSHOFF
Production Coordinator . . . PATTY WILLETT
Assistant Production Coordinator
. . . . CHRISTINE PUTNAM
Production Secretary . . . . . JODI ARNESON
Travel Coordinator . . . . JILL VAUPEN
Dialect Coach . . . . TIM MONICH
Choreographer. . . . . JOANN JENSEN
Acting Coach . . . . HAROLD GUSKIN
Archival Footage . . . . DEBORAH RICKETTS
Unit Publicist . . . . JAMES FERRERA
Assistant to Mr. Schamus . . . . FELIPE TEWES
Assistant to Ms. Costas . . . . . . JESSE LIOTTA
Assistant to Mr. Lee . . . . CATHERINE SHAO
Assistant to Mr. Hausman
. . . . EMILY EVASHEVSKI
Office Production Assistants
. . . . MATT ANDERSON
JOHN EDMUNDSON
ETHAN DUFFY
Asset Production Assistant
. . . . THOMAS LOMBARDI
Film Runner . . . . DANIEL BISBING
Environmental Steward . . . . NICOLE FEDER
Production Interns . . . . . . NICO BRUGGE
ADAM DUDEK
MICHAEL FORDES
ALEXANDER FRIEDMAN
HARRY ISRAELSON
ANNALISA SHOEMAKER
Second Second Assistant Director
. . . . TUDOR JONES
DGA Trainee . . . . MAURA KELLY
Key Set Production Assistant. . CHRIS GIBSON
First Team Production Assistant
. . . . MONICA ESTRADA
Background Production Assistant
. . . . CASEY MADIGAN
Vehicles Production Assistant
. . . . SCOTT FOSTER
Walkie Production Assistant
. . . . MICHAEL COAST
Set Production Assistants
. . . . CRISTAL CALDERON
VINCENT GIARRATANO
SCOTT BOWERS
TIMOTHY S. KANE
RAMONA MURPHY-ADAIR
CHRIS RYAN
TEDDY CECIL
Graphic Designer. . . . . DAWN MASI
Art Department Coordinator . . ERIK KNIGHT

Illustrator . . . . JAVIER AMEIJEIRAS	ADR Recorded at . . . . SOUND ONE CORP
Assistant Set Decorator . . . . . . BECCA MEIS	DE LANE LEA LTD.
DEMARCO	P.O.P SOUND
Second Assistant Set Decorator	ADR Voice Casting. . . . . . SONDRA JAMES
. . . . SUSAN KAUFMAN	Post Production Sound Facility . . . . . C5, INC.
Leadman. . . . . DICK TICE	Re-Recordists. . . . . DROR GESCHEIT
On Set Dressers. . . . . . . ARI SCHWARTZ	HARRY HIGGINS
JOSH CLARK	Mix Technicians . . . . AVI LANIADO
Set Dressers . . . . MIKE BOUCHER	BOB TROELLER
DUNCAN E. BRYANT	Re-Recording Mixers . . . . . REILLY STEELE
NICK FERRARA	EUGENE GEARTY
JOAN FINLAY	Mixed at . . . . SOUND ONE CORP.
CHRIS HEAPS	Location Manager . . . . JOE C. GUEST
BRIAN JONES	Key Assistant Location Manager . . GUY EFRAT
MIKE KOVAL	Assistant Location Manager
HELEN RIPPLE	. . . . SETH BLACKMAN
JACK BRANDT	Pre-Production Assistant Location Manager
CARL FERRARA	. . . . MATT KANIA
CHRIS FERRARO	Location Assistants . . PHUONG-THUY PHAM
CHRIS GRANO	SARAH FOLLETT
JON HOPKINS	MARA ALCALY
CLIFF KLATT	ROBERT NOONAN
KEVIN LEONIDAS	Location Scouts . . . . . . LAURA BERNING
BRUCE SWANSON	BILL GARVEY
Set Decoration Production Assistant	JASON FRITZ
. . . . IMOGEN LEE	DAVID McGUIRE
Art Department Production Assistants	Unit Assistants . . . . ABI JACKSON
. . . . LIZA DONATELLI	RUFUS WYER
NELL TIVNAN	Production Accountant. . . . . JOYCE HSIEH
Tailor . . . . JARED LEESE	First Assistant Accountant . . . . JACK BAVARO
Ager/Dyer. . . . . DAVID PAULIN	Payroll Accountant . . . . LINDA TOON
Costume Coordinator . . . JESSICA PITCAIRN	Second Assistant Accountants
Costume Production Assistants	. . . . . LISA MARIE MADDEN-CORRADO
. . . . PATRICK JAMES LEACH	SANTENA JENARIS KING
JESSICA TREJOS	Additional Payroll. . . . . TESSIE TAN
BRIANA DESIREE MAGNIFICO	Accounting Clerks . . . . ABBY COON
Supervising Sound Editors . . EUGENE GEARTY	WILL O'DWYER
PHILIP STOCKTON	Post Production Accountant
Sound Effects Editor . . . . WYATT SPRAGUE	. . . . YANA COLLINS LEHMAN
Dialogue Editor . . . . . . PHILIP STOCKTON	TREVANNA POST
ADR Supervisor . . . . KENTON JAKUB	Key Video Assist. . . . . JOEL HOLLAND
First Assistant Sound Editor . . CHRIS FIELDER	Additional Video Assist
FX Assistant. . . . . LARRY WINELAND	. . . . ANDREW CAVAGNET
Foley Supervisor . . . . . . REUBEN SIMON	Construction Coordinator. . . . NICK MILLER
Music Editor . . . . E. GEDNEY WEBB	Key Shop Craftsperson
Assistant Music Editor . . . . ERIC PAUL	. . . . GORDON S. KRAUSE
Foley Engineer . . . . . . GEORGE A. LARA	Foreman Shop Craftspersons
Foley Artist . . . . . . MARKO COSTANZO	. . . . ROBERT A. VACCARIELLO
ADR Mixers . . . . BOBBY JOHANSON	ROBERT DiGRIGOLI
PETER GLEAVES	Shop Craftspersons . . . . DERRICK ALFORD
MICHAEL MILLER	CHUCK WHITNEY
ADR Recordists. . . . . . . MIKE HOWELLS	KEN BRZOZOWSKI
RICK GOULD	JOHN CODA
COURTNEY BISHOP	JOHN R. JOHNSTON

Shop Craftspersons (cont.)
. . . . RAYMOND REDDY
KEVIN ROACH
BETSY TANNER
Key Construction Electric – New Lebanon
. . . . RICHARD FORD
Key Construction Electric – Yonkers
. . . . LANCE SHEPHERD
Key Construction Grip
. . . . JONATHAN GRAHAM
Best Boy Construction Grips
. . . . KENNETH J. BURKE
TIMOTHY MONTGOMERY
Construction Grips . . . TODD MacNICHOLL
KEVIN MONTGOMERY
MELVIN NOPED
JAMES REID
THOMAS WALKER
DANIEL WOODS
Construction Production Assistant
. . . . TOM BERNINGER
Master Scenic Artist . . . . . ROBERT TOPOL
Camera Scenic . . . . . . M. TONY TROTTA
Scenic Foreperson . . . . . . DIANE P. RICH
Scenic Shopperson . . . . . . IOANNIS ZAPTIS
Scenics . . . . RAND ANGELICOLA
YONGXI CHEN
STEPHEN CALDWELL
MAGGIE RYAN
JUDIE JURACEK
CATHY COLBY-GRAUER
MARK BACHMAN
COLT HAUSMAN
Greens Coordinator . . . . WILL SCHECK
Greens Foreman . . . . . GORDON GERTSEN
Stand By Greensman . . . . PEDRO BARQUIN
Greens . . . . FRAZER NEWTON
JIM COOK
MIKE THOMPSON
ARLO HOFFMAN
Parking Coordinator . . . . . KERRY CLARK
Security Coordinators
. . . . PAT SHANAHAN, GMCS, Inc.
KEVIN CHENEY, GMCS, Inc.
Parking/Security Production Assistants
. . . . FREDDY GERMOSEN
SEAN McMILLAN
BORIS GONSALES
MICHELLE HAVLICEK
ISMAEL HENDRICKS
DEANE SOUTHWORTH
GERALD LOWE
Insurance Provided by
. . . . AON/ALBERT G. RUBEN

Legal Services provided by . . . . . SHEPPARD
MULLIN RICHTER & HAMPTON, LLP
Clearance Services Provided by
. . . . ASHLEY KRAVITZ,
CLEARED BY ASHLEY, INC.
Product Placement . . . . . EMILY GANNETT
Music Legal and Clearances by
. . . . CHRISTINE BERGREN
Picture Car Coordinator
. . . . PHILIP SCHNEIDER
Picture Car Assistants . . . . LEWIS ZUCKER
KIP BARTLETT
Picture Car Mechanic . . . . . . JUNJI ITAGAKI
Picture Car Production Assistant
. . . . BIFFY CAHILL
Transportation Captain . . JAMES P. WHALEN
Transportation Co-Captain
. . . . JOSEPH J. BUONOCORE, JR.
Driver for Mr. Lee . . . . HERB LIEBERZ
15 Passenger Van #1 . . . . SCOTT BUCCIERO
15 Passenger Van #2 . . . . . . MIKE LAMORA
15 Passenger Van #3 . . . . . JERRY MOSKAL
Mr. Lee/Production Trailer . . . . TOM BAKER
DOT Dispatcher
. . . . WILLIAM MIKE BUCKMAN
Set Dressing Truck . . . . ROY FORTIER
Swing Truck . . . . RICH O'CONNELL
Greens Truck . . . . . . TIMOTHY CARROLL
Construction Stake . . . . . . MIKE DINARDO
Car Carrier . . . . DAVE KRUK
Hair/MU Trailer . . . . JOSEPH RISO
Honeywagon Driver . . . . JOHN BLACK
Cast Trailer . . . . RYAN COOKE
Wardrobe Trailer . . . . . WILLIAM ESPANET
Grip Trailer . . . . ANDREW COLLINS
Electric Trailer . . . . PAUL WIENER
Camera Trailer . . . . MATT MAMOLA
Prop Trailer . . . . . . RUEBEN TOMPKINS
SFX Trailer . . . . MIKE BELLAMARE
Set Decorator Van . . . . ED FOX
Casting Associates . . . . . LEEBA ZAKHAROV
LOIS DRABKIN
Casting Assistant . . . . MATTHEW HONOVIC
Extras Casting . . . . . . SOPHIA M. COSTAS
Extras Casting . . SHAUN CARROLL DUFFY
Extras Casting Assistants . . LINDSEY ROBERTS
JOLANDA ANTHONY
Extras Casting Production Assistants . . . .
AINSLEY BARTHOLOMEW
SOPHIE CHAMINO
SPENCER MONDSHEIN
ROBERT WEDGE
Horse Trainer . . . . CARI SWANSON

Tisha's Yorkie . . "HESKETHANE TALLULAH
BANKHEAD"
Yorkie Owner . . . . KAREN HUDSON
Quail Wrangler . . . . STEVE McAULIFF,
ANIMAL ACTORS INT. INC.
Catering . . . . . . FOR STARS CATERING
Caterer . . . . LLOYD THOMAS
Cook/Driver . . . . EMMANUEL REYES
Cooks . . . . BEN HAMMER
JOSEPH BENEDETTO
Assistants . . . . HUGO ZEPEDA
WHITNEY BRANN
First Aid . . . . RICHARD FELLEGARA
KATHY FELLEGARA
JONATHAN ELLIS
Tutor . . . . CATHERINE TERESCO
Craft Service . . . . WILSON RIVAS
Craft Service Assistants
. . . . DIEGO QUIRIMDUNBAY
PEDRO GARCIA
Visual Effects by MR. X INC.
Visual Effects Supervisor
. . . . BRENDAN TAYLOR
Senior Visual Effects Producer
. . . . DENNIS BERARDI
Visual Effects Producer
. . . . COLLEEN JENKINSON
Visual Effects Coordinators
. . . . DOUG MELVILLE
MELANIE MARTIN
Pipeline Supervisor . . . AARON WEINTRAUB
Lead Compositor . . . . KRIS CARSON
Digital Compositors
. . . . MATHIEU ARCHAMBAULT
MICHELLE ASTRUG
BARB BENOIT
HARSHAL BHUJBAL
WAYNE BRINTON
DOMINIK BOCHENSKI
ZAC CAMPBELL
TOMMASO CORONA
RICHARD CHIU
JAMES COOPER
OVIDIU CINAZAN
ANIRBAN DAS
ROBERTO D'IPPOLITO
THAI SON DOAN
DANNY DUCHESNEAU
AMELIE DUBOIS
NICK FAIRHEAD
MATT GREENWOOD
ANNA JOUKOVA
VIKRAM KALE
SAMEER KUDALE

MIKE KWAN
NIKHIL LONKAR
NITIN MAHAJAN
CLAIRE McLACHLAN
PETE O'CONNELL
HOJIN PARK
SEBASTIEN PROULX
KEVIN QUATMAN
PAUL SAINT-HILAIRE
BHUSHAN HUMBE
KENNY SALES
MAG SARNOWSKA
VINOD SATHE
JERRY SEGUIN
CAROLYN SHELBY
KYLE SIM
TAMARA STONE
ABU TAHIR
BRIDGET TAYLOR
SEBASTIEN VEILLEUX
GWEN ZHANG
Digital Matte Painting . . . MATT SCHOFIELD
MATTHEW BORRETT
KEN McCUEN
Modeling & Texturing . . . JASON GOUGEON
SEAN MILLS
JACKSON LI
Lighting Supervisor . . . . DOMINIC REMANE
Lighting . . . . MANDY AU
GUSTAVO FERNANDES
Technical Supervisor . . . . . . BEN SIMONS
Effects Animation . . . . . JEREMY DINEEN
Shader Writers . . . . . . JAMES GOODMAN
JIM PRICE
Animation Lead . . . . . DANIEL MIZUGUSHI
Animation . . . . DAN CARNEGIE
CHRIS DE SOUZA
HUBERT CHAN
PETE DYDO
ETHAN LEE
MATT RALPH
ABHISHEK SAXENA
GAVIN SOARES
JIM SU
Production Management
. . . . ISABELLE LANGLOIS
SARAH BARBER
CHEYENNE BLOOMFIELD
JESH KRISHNA MURTHY
ROOPESH GUJAR
AMOD DIWAKAR
Assistant Visual Effects Producer
. . . . WILSON CAMERON
Dailies Operator . . . . ROB PHILLIPS

Production Assistants . . . . TOMMY GERVAIS
SAFIA SIAD
Digital Intermediate by
. . . . DELUXE NEW YORK
Digital Intermediate Colorist
. . . . JOSEPH GAWLER
Digital Intermediate Editor
. . . . JACOB ROBINSON
Digital Intermediate Coordinator
. . . . DARRELL R. SMITH
Digital Intermediate Assist
. . . . JONATHAN SANDEN
JACK LEWARS
Smoke Artist . . . . . . CHRIS MACKENZIE
Scanning & Recording . . . MARKUS JANNER
Data Wrangler . . . . . DUCK GROSSBERG
QC Lead. . . . . MOLLE DeBARTOLO
Video Master Colorist . . . . . JOHN POTTER
Dailies Colorist . . . . STEVEN BODNER, JR.
Dailies Project Manager . . . . . JEFF HOCKEN
Dqailies Colorist Assist
. . . . THOMAS CENTRONE
KEVIN KROUT
Engineering . . . . TIM MULLEN
DAVID CHAI
HD Avids provided by . . . . PIVOTAL POST
Editing Rooms provided by . . POST FACTORY
Arcade Games provided by . . MICKEY TREAT
Titles by . . . . yU & co
Color Timer. . . . . DAVE PULTZ
Dolby Sound Consultant . . STEVE F.B. SMITH
Music Engineer
. . . . LAWRENCE MANCHESTER
Klezmer Clarinet . . . . . DAVID KRAKAUER
Background Music Effects . . . DANNY SABER
Music Supervisor . . . . JOE BOYD

SONGS

How Could We Know
Written by Jamie Dunlap, Stephen Lang
and Scott Nickoley
Performed by Lori Mark
Courtesy of Marc Ferrari/Mastersource

Stoned on the Range
Written and Performed by Don Puglisi

No Love, No Nothin'
Written by Leo Feist and Harry Warren
Performed by Judy Garland

Courtesy of Geffen Records
Under License from Universal Music Enterprises

Wispy Paisley Skies
Written by Warren Klein
Performed by Fraternity of Men
Courtesy of Geffen Records
Under license from Universal Music Enterprises

Maggie M'Gill
Written by John Densmore, Robert Krieger,
Raymond Manzarek and Jim Morrison
Performed by The Doors
Courtesy of Elektra Entertainment Group
By arrangement with Warner Music Group Film
& TV Licensing

No Escape
Written by Sky Saxon, Jimmy Lawrence
and Jan Larson
Performed by The Seeds
Courtesy of GNP Crescendo Records
By arrangement with Ocean Park Music Group

Motherless Child
Written by Fred Herrera and Nancy Nevins
Performed by Sweetwater
Courtesy of Warner Bros. Records Inc.
By arrangement with Warner Music Group Film
& TV Licensing

One More Mile
Written by James Cotton
Performed by The Paul Butterfield Blues Band
Courtesy of Elektra Entertainment Group
By arrangement with Warner Music Group Film
& TV Licensing

Do Wah Diddy Diddy
Written by Jeff Barry and Ellie Greenwich
Performed by Hairy Pretzel

Wooden Ships
Written by David Crosby, Paul Kantner and
Stephen Stills
Performed by Crosby, Stills & Nash
Courtesy of Atlantic Recording Corp.
By arrangement with Warner Music Group Film
& TV Licensing

Flutes, Bongos & Limbos
Written by Dan Knobler, Gaston Jean-Baptiste,
Jon Seale and Michael McGinnis
Performed by El Monaco Bar Band

The Flute & Bongo Sizzle
Written by Dan Knobler, Gaston Jean-Baptiste,
Jon Seale and Michael McGinnis
Performed by El Monaco Bar Band

Hare Krishna Maha Mantra
Written and performed by International Society
for Krishna Consciousness Boston Devotees
Courtesy of ISKCON of New England

Handsome Johnny
Written by Louis Gossett, Jr. and Richard Havens
Performed by Richie Havens
Courtesy of Stormy Forest Productions Inc.
By arrangement with Bug Music

China Cat Sunflower
Written by Jerry Garcia and Robert Hunter
Performed by Grateful Dead
Courtesy of Warner Bros. Records Inc.
By arrangement with Warner Music Group Film
& TV Licensing

High Flyin' Bird
Written by Billy Edd Wheeler
Performed by Richie Havens
Courtesy of Stormy Forest Productions Inc.
By arrangement with Bug Music

Beautiful People
Written by Melanie Safka
Performed by Melanie
Courtesy of Buddah Records and The RCA/Jive
Label Group, a unit of Sony Music Entertainment
By arrangement with Sony Music Entertainment

Coming Into Los Angeles
Written and performed by Arlo Guthrie
Courtesy of Warner Bros. Entertainment Inc.

America
Written by Paul Simon
Produced by Sourcerer
Performed by Ken Strange, Jeff Paris and Bob Hackl

If I Were a Carpenter
Written and performed by Tim Hardin
Courtesy of Universal Records
Under license from Universal Music Enterprises

Red Telephone
Written by Arthur Lee
Performed by Love
Courtesy of Elektra Entertainment Group
By arrangement with Warner Music Group Film
& TV Licensing

Mind Flowers
Written by Ian Bruce-Douglas
Performed by Ultimate Spinach
Courtesy of Iris Properties, Inc.

Raga Manj Khamaj
Written by Ali Akbar Khan and Ravi Shankar
Performed by Ravi Shankar
Courtesy of Capitol Records
Under license from EMI Film & Television Music

Sweet Sir Galahad
Written and performed by Joan Baez
Courtesy of Vanguard Records, A Welk Music
Group Company

I Feel Like I'm Fixin' To Die Rag
Written by Joe McDonald
Performed by Country Joe and the Fish
Courtesy of Rag Baby Records Company

I Shall Be Released
Written by Bob Dylan
Performed by The Band
Courtesy of Capitol Records
By arrangement with EMI Film & Television
Music

Going Up the Country
Written by Alan Wilson
Performed by Canned Heat
Courtesy of Capitol Records
Under license from EMI Film & Television Music

Try (Just a Little Bit Harder)
Written by Jerry Ragovoy and Chip Taylor
Performed by Janis Joplin
Courtesy of Janet Joplin Estate

Essen
Written by Lee Tully and S. Demay

Can't Find My Way Home
Written by Steve Winwood
Performed by Steve Winwood
Courtesy of Wincraft Music, Inc.

Volunteers
Written by Martyn J. Buchwald and Paul Kantner
Performed by Jefferson Airplane
Courtesy of The RCA Records Label and The
RCA/Jive Label Group, a unit of Sony Music
Entertainment
By arrangement with Sony Music Entertainment

Freedom (2009)
Written by Richard Havens
Performed by Richie Havens
Courtesy of Stormy Forest Productions Inc.
By arrangement with Bug Music

The pages from The Times Herald-Record in this
movie are modifications of the pages published in
1969 and do not necessarily reflect the dates, pages
and/or photographs as they actually appeared in
The Times-Herald at the time.

WOODSTOCK®, 3 DAYS OF PEACE &
MUSIC®, and the Dove and Guitar Logo®, are
trademarks of Woodstock Ventures LC and are
used under License.

'Sweet Charity' & 'Topaz' posters courtesy of
Universal Studios Licensing LLLP

Stock Footage Courtesy of
BBC Motion Gallery
NBC News Archives
ABCNews Videosource
NASA

Stock Photographs Courtesy of Corbis

American Humane monitored some of the animal
action. No animals were harmed in those scenes.
(AHAD 01381)

This motion picture used sustainability strategies to
reduce its carbon emissions and environmental
impact

For more information visit
www.filminfocus.com/goGreen

Special Thanks
New York State Governor's Office for Motion
Picture & Television Development
New York City Mayor's Office of Film, Theatre &
Broadcasting

New York State Department of Transportation –
Region 8 & Region 1

The New York State Office of Parks, Recreation
and Historic Preservation and Cherry Plain State
Park

The New York State Police
New York State Thruway Authority

The People of COLUMBIA COUNTY
Columbia County Tourism Department
Columbia County Sheriff's Office

Town of NEW LEBANON, NY
Lebanon Valley Business Association
New Lebanon Central School District

Towns of STEPHENTOWN, CHATHAM,
HILLSDALE, MILLERTON, SCHODACK, and
Hamlet of EAST CHATHAM, NY

Martin Scorsese

Alan Horn

Margaret Bodde
Jennifer Ahn

MPAA #45200

ABOUT THE FILMMAKERS

ANG LEE (Director/Producer) Taiwan-born Ang Lee is one of the world's most revered and honored film directors. He has won 2 Academy Awards (in 2006, for his Direction of *Brokeback Mountain*, and in 2001, for Best Foreign-Language Film for *Crouching Tiger, Hidden Dragon*). His films have twice won the prestigious Golden Lion Award for Best Picture at the Venice International Film Festival (in 2007, for *Lust, Caution*, and in 2005, for *Brokeback Mountain*) and twice won the Golden Bear for Best Film at the Berlin International Film Festival (in 1993, for *The Wedding Banquet* and in 1996, for *Sense and Sensibility*). His most recent film, *Lust, Caution*, swept Asia's Golden Horse Awards (Taiwan's equivalent of the Academy Awards), with 8 wins including Best Film; it is one of the highest-grossing and most critically acclaimed films in the history of Chinese-language cinema.

Brokeback Mountain won 2 additional Academy Awards – Best Adapted Screenplay (Larry McMurtry & Diana Ossana) and Best Original Score (Gustavo Santaolalla) – and was nominated for 5 more, including Best Picture. Mr. Lee also won the Directors Guild of America, BAFTA, Independent Spirit, and Golden Globe Awards for Best Director, among other industry accolades. The film won 3 additional Golden Globe Awards, including Best Picture [Drama]; the Independent Spirit Award for Best Feature; 3 additional BAFTA Awards, including Best Film; and the Golden Lion Award, for Best Picture, at the 2005 Venice International Film Festival, among awards all over the world.

Additionally, Mr. Lee and the film's star Jake Gyllenhaal were honored with the Human Rights Campaign Equality Award;

and *Brokeback Mountain* was named Outstanding Film [Wide Release] by the Gay & Lesbian Alliance Against Defamation's (GLAAD) Media Awards.

Crouching Tiger, Hidden Dragon, based on a novel by Du Lu Wang, won 3 additional Academy Awards – Best Cinematography (Peter Pau), Best Original Score (Tan Dun), and Best Art Direction/Set Decoration (Tim Yip) – and was nominated for 6 more, including Best Picture and Best Director. Mr. Lee won the Directors Guild of America, BAFTA, and Golden Globe Awards for Best Director, among other honors.

Mr. Lee moved to the United States in 1978. After receiving a Bachelor of Fine Arts in theatre from the University of Illinois, he went to New York University to complete a Masters of Fine Arts Degree in film production. His short film *Fine Line* won Best Director and Best Film awards at the annual NYU Film Festival.

His first feature film, *Pushing Hands*, was screened at the 1992 Berlin International Film Festival and won Best Film at the Asian-Pacific Film Festival. The film was also nominated for 9 Golden Horse Awards.

Pushing Hands was also the first film in his "Father Knows Best" trilogy, all of which starred actor Sihung Lung. The next film in the trilogy, *The Wedding Banquet*, opened following its Berlin premiere and prize to international acclaim. The film was nominated for the Academy Award and the Golden Globe Award for Best Foreign-Language Film, and received 6 Independent Spirit Award nominations. Mr. Lee capped the trilogy with *Eat Drink Man Woman*, which was selected as the opening night feature for the Directors Fortnight section of the 1994 Cannes International Film Festival. Named Best Foreign-Language Film by the National Board of Review, the film was nominated for the Academy Award and the Golden Globe Award for Best Foreign-Language Film, and received 6 Independent Spirit Award nominations.

In 1995, he directed *Sense and Sensibility*, starring Emma Thompson and Kate Winslet. The film was nominated for 7 Academy Awards, including Best Picture, and won for Best Adapted Screenplay (Emma Thompson, from the Jane Austen novel). *Sense and Sensibility* also won Golden Globe Awards for Best Picture [Drama] and Best Screenplay; and was named Best Picture by BAFTA, the Boston Society of Film Critics, and the National Board of Review. Mr. Lee was cited as Best Director by the New York Film Critics Circle, the National Board of Review, and the Boston Society of Film Critics.

Mr. Lee next directed *The Ice Storm*, adapted by James Schamus from Rick Moody's novel, and starring Joan Allen, Kevin Kline, Sigourney Weaver, Christina Ricci, and Tobey Maguire. The film premiered at the 1997 Cannes International Film Festival (where it won the Best Screenplay award), and was selected as the opening night feature for the 1997 New York Film Festival. For her performance in the film, Sigourney Weaver won a BAFTA Award, and was nominated for a Golden Globe Award, for Best Supporting Actress.

Mr. Lee's subsequent films were *Ride with the Devil* (adapted by James Schamus from Daniel Woodrell's novel, again starring Tobey Maguire); *Crouching Tiger, Hidden Dragon*; the boxoffice hit *The Hulk* (starring Eric Bana and Jennifer Connelly); and, for Focus Features, *Brokeback Mountain* and *Lust, Caution*.

In addition to the Venice prize, the latter film's other honors included Independent Spirit Award nominations for lead actors Tony Leung and Tang Wei; Ms. Tang also earned a BAFTA Award nomination. The film was a nominee in the Foreign-Language Film category from both the BAFTA and Golden Globe Awards.

JAMES SCHAMUS (Screenwriter/ Producer) James Schamus is chief executive officer (CEO) of Focus Features. Focus Features and Focus Features International (FFI) together comprise a singular global company, dedicated to producing, acquiring, financing, selling, and distributing original and daring films from emerging and established filmmakers – films that challenge mainstream moviegoers to embrace and enjoy voices and visions from around the world. The company's flexible and nuanced approach to distribution allows it to support a wide range of films, from those geared to a single local market to worldwide hits. The company operates as Focus Features domestically, and as Focus Features International overseas.

An integral contributor to the American independent film business for over two decades, Mr. Schamus has the unique distinction of being an award-winning screenwriter and producer who is also a film executive.

Mr. Schamus formed Focus with David Linde in May 2002. Prior to the formation of Focus, Mr. Schamus was co-president of the independent film production company Good Machine, which he co-founded in 1991. Mr. Schamus and his partners at the company produced over 40 films during an 11-year period, in partnership with filmmakers such as Ang Lee, Todd Solondz, and Nicole Holofcener. Through its financing and distribution arm, Good Machine International, the company represented dozens more filmmakers, among them Pedro Almodóvar and the Coen Brothers. Good Machine was honored with a 10-year retrospective at the Museum of Modern Art in New York City.

Mr. Schamus is also a screenwriter, and received Academy Award nominations in the Best Adapted Screenplay and Best Original Song categories for his work on Ang Lee's *Crouching Tiger, Hidden Dragon.* The blockbuster Good Machine feature, which Mr. Schamus co-wrote and executive-produced, won 4 Academy Awards.

Mr. Schamus has had a long collaboration as writer and producer with Ang Lee on eleven feature films, with the director's *Brokeback Mountain,* starring Heath Ledger and Jake Gyllenhaal, released worldwide through Focus Features. The film is Focus' all-time top-grosser, with global ticket sales of over $180 million. *Brokeback Mountain,* on which Mr. Schamus served as a producer, won, among other honors, 3 Academy Awards; 4 Golden Globe Awards; 4 BAFTA Awards; and the Producers Guild of America's top prize, the [Darryl F. Zanuck] Producer of the Year Award, Theatrical Motion Pictures.

Their other films together include *Lust, Caution* (which Mr. Schamus co-wrote and produced, and which won the Golden Lion Award for Best Picture at the 2007 Venice International Film Festival), released worldwide by Focus; *The Hulk* (which Mr. Schamus wrote and produced); *Ride with the Devil* (which Mr. Schamus produced and adapted); *The Ice Storm* (which Mr. Schamus produced and adapted, earning the Best Screenplay prize at the 1997 Cannes International Film Festival as well as WGA and BAFTA Award nominations); *Sense and Sensibility* (which Mr. Schamus co-produced); *Eat Drink Man Woman* (which Mr. Schamus co-wrote and associate-produced); *The Wedding Banquet* (which Mr. Schamus co-wrote and produced); and *Pushing Hands* (which Mr. Schamus produced).

Mr. Schamus executive-produced several Good Machine features that won the Grand Jury Prize at the Sundance Film Festival, including Edward Burns' *The Brothers McMullen,* Tom Noonan's *What Happened Was...,* and Todd Haynes' *Poison.* Among the other films that he executive-produced at Good Machine are Paul Schrader's *AutoFocus,* Gregor Jordan's *Buffalo Soldiers,* Todd Solondz' *Happiness,* Bart Freundlich's *The Myth of Fingerprints,* Cindy Sherman's *Office Killer,* Nicole Holofcener's *Walking and Talking,* and Todd Haynes' *Safe.*

He is also Professor in Columbia University's School of the Arts, where he teaches film history and theory; and he currently serves on the board of directors of Creative Capital. He was the 2006 Presidential Fellow in the Humanities at the University of Chicago, and received his Ph.D. in English from U.C. Berkeley in 2003.

Mr. Schamus was honored with the NBC Screenwriter Tribute at the 2002 Nantucket Film Festival as well as with the Writers Guild of America, East's 2003 Richard B. Jablow Award for devoted service to the Guild.

Focus' celebrated releases have included seven more Academy Award winners: Gus Van Sant's *Milk,* Sofia Coppola's *Lost in Translation* (which grossed over $100 million worldwide), Roman Polanski's *The Pianist,* Fernando Meirelles' *The Constant Gardener,* Michel Gondry's *Eternal Sunshine of the Spotless Mind,* Walter Salles' *The Motorcycle Diaries,* and Joe Wright's *Atonement;* and Cary Joji Fukunaga's *Sin Nombre,* Henry Selick's *Coraline,* Joel and Ethan Coen's *Burn After Reading* (which grossed over $155 million worldwide), Martin McDonagh's *In Bruges,* Joe Wright's *Pride & Prejudice,* Todd Haynes' *Far from Heaven,* François Ozon's *Swimming Pool,* and Alejandro González Iñárritu's *21 Grams.*